The Curious Case of Charlie Peace

James Tierney

Copyright © 2017 James Tierney
All rights reserved.
ISBN: 9781520441207
ISBN-13: 9781520441207

DEDICATION

For May and Jimmy.

CONTENTS

1 Chapter One 01
2 Chapter Two 12
3 Chapter Three 19
4 Chapter Four 28
5 Chapter Five 48
6 Chapter Six 56
7 Chapter Seven 73
8 Chapter Eight 80

ACKNOWLEDGMENTS

With thanks to the National Library of Scotland for access to their extensive records.

CHAPTER ONE

It was 2am on Thursday 10 October 1878. The night was still and the stray cats were on the prowl, as Metropolitan Police-Constable Edward Robinson made his way down the avenue leading from St John's Park to Blackheath.

As he passed the rear of the second house in the street, Robinson's eyes were drawn to a faint, flickering, light emitting from the drawing-room window. At any other time, Robinson may have given little thought to the source of the light, but the London police were on heightened alert, due to an epidemic of daring, unsolved, burglaries that had recently spread around the affluent area of Blackheath, causing consternation among the well-heeled local house-owners.

The police had received regular weekly reports of burglaries but, despite their best efforts, they had failed to discover the identity of the perpetrator. All they had been able to ascertain was the chief suspect had very small feet, traces of small boot-marks having been invariably found in the gardens of the houses broken into.

Robinson decided to investigate further. Firstly, he sought the assistance of a fellow constable he knew to be close by. He attracted the attention of Police-Constable William Girling and the two policemen fixed their focus on the dull light steadily moving from the drawing-room of the property into several other sections of the house.

Girling hoisted Robinson onto the garden wall surrounding the property, before he, himself, was helped onto the wall by another officer drawn to the scene, Police-Sergeant Charles Brown. With his two fellow officers in place, Brown moved to the front of the house and rang the doorbell.

As soon as the doorbell was sounded, the faint light that had first attracted the policemen's attention was extinguished. Shortly thereafter, a shadowy figure emerged from the drawing-room window, which opened onto the garden lawn. Robinson launched himself from the garden wall onto the lawn, whilst Girling jumped into the avenue.

As he landed on the lawn, Robinson's foot stamped down on a broken bottle hidden beneath the wall. The sound alerted the mystery man who'd climbed from the window and he took flight towards the bottom of the garden. Robinson took chase. The policeman, who was much greater in stature than his prey, quickly closed the gap between them. His progress came to a shuddering halt when his eyes fixed upon the barrel of the revolver now pointing directly at his head.

The constable stood barely six yards away from the man, whose misshapen figure was highlighted in the glow of the full moon.

'Keep back, keep off, or by God, I will shoot you,' the man said.

'Don't be stupid, you've been caught and others are with me,' the policeman replied, in a steady and confident voice.

The words had barely left his mouth before three thunderous sounds rung in his ears, as two bullets flew past the left side of his head and another passed just above. As the shots whistled by, Robinson, with little regard for his own safety, rushed towards the gunman and was greeted by a further shot flying past the right side of his head. Having now fully closed the gap between them, the policeman landed a clubbing blow on the man's face with his left fist, while trying to protect his own head with his right hand.

'You bastard, I will settle you this time,' the man cried out, before firing a shot that blasted through the policeman's right arm.

As blood sprayed from the wound above his elbow, Robinson threw himself upon the shooter and the two men crashed to the ground. The man was not for giving up and said, 'You bastard, I'll give you something else to think about,' as his left hand reached towards his pocket.

Thankfully, Robinson managed to get a firm grip on the gunman's arm, which he quickly twisted, before grabbing hold of the revolver and smashing it into the man's head. Robinson found the revolver was actually strapped around the man's wrist, but he didn't allow this to deter him as he rained down a series of blows, using the revolver and the man's own fist.

Turning him over and pressing his face firmly into the ground, Robinson held his prisoner in position with his knee and his left hand, until help finally arrived in the shape of Sergeant Brown. Constable Girling followed close behind and got there just as Robinson was beginning to feel the effects of his wound and was struggling to retain consciousness.

'I am struck through the arm Girling,' Robinson cried out.

Girling assisted his fellow constable by holding the captured man down. Sergeant Brown noticed a six-chamber revolver lay close to the man's hand and, unaware the gun was still strapped to the prone prisoner's wrist, brought his truncheon crashing down on the man's fingers. The prisoner squealed in pain as Brown eventually wrenched the strapping from his wrist.

'I've got hold of him Edward,' Girling declared, 'you'd better get to the station and have your arm dressed.'

As Robinson climbed unsteadily to his feet, the captured man muttered to Girling, 'I only meant to frighten him, to get away.'

As the subdued prisoner lay groaning on the ground, Sergeant Brown carried out a search of the surrounding area to ascertain whether the man had any accomplices, but nobody else was found.

Brown and Constable Girling then turned their attention to searching the prisoner. The man's pockets contained a silver pocket-flask, a banker's cheque-book, a letter-case and a small crow-bar. The man was also carrying several potential house-breaking implements, including an auger, a centre-bit, a small hand-vice, two knives, a gimlet and three screws, among other items.

When Girling pulled the prisoner to his feet, the man made one last futile effort to escape, only to be thwarted by a crushing blow from the constable's truncheon. Girling escorted his prisoner to the Greenwich police station-house, while Brown knocked on the door of the house at 2 St John's Park, owned by Mr James Alexander Burness. Brown was granted entry by one of the servants, Sarah Cooper.

Inside the dining-room, Brown found the window was open and, on a nearby table, some plate, a crumb scoop, a sugar-basin, a silver spoon and a decanter lay ready for collection. It seemed clear the burglar had been disturbed before he had been able to package the items for removal.

Sarah Cooper advised the policeman that, when she had gone to bed at around 10pm the previous night, the house had been secured and the doors and windows had all been fastened.

Brown and Cooper were soon joined by Police Inspector John Body, who carried out his own search of the property and noted marks on the dining-room window that appeared to have been made by a jemmy. The window had been forced open, the catch having been sprung.

A hole, about five inches wide, had been cut through the dining-room door. The hole was large enough to allow a man's hand to be pushed through, to unlock the door from the other side. Inside the library, the Inspector found a desk had been forced open and the drawers of a chiffonier had also been forced.

Following their search of the property, the two policemen returned to the station-house and Body formally entered charges against the prisoner, for breaking into and entering the property at 2 St John's Park, Blackheath, for the purpose of burglary, and for shooting Police-Constable Robinson with a revolver, with intent to murder him.

The prisoner offered no response when the charges were read to him and in reply to Body's request to provide his name and address, merely said, 'Why don't you find out for yourself?'

The following morning, the unnamed prisoner was brought before the magistrate at the Greenwich Police Court. The prisoner was described as a half-caste, aged around sixty and of singular appearance. The only information the man had provided to the police was that he had only been in the country for a short time. He was remanded for a week, to allow the police to carry out further inquiries.

The first clue the police uncovered regarding the identity of their prisoner was when they intercepted a letter he had tried to smuggle out, addressed to a 'Mrs Thompson' and signed 'John Ward'.

It had not gone unnoticed that, following the arrest of 'John Ward', the burglary count in the Blackheath area had dropped to near zero. Police attention was focused on locating Mrs Thompson and finding out all they could about 'John Ward'. It was quickly discovered the prisoner had been living in seemingly respectable circumstances, under the name Thompson, with a woman he had represented to be his wife. The couple had been running a business as musical instrument dealers.

When the police arrived at the Thompson household, the premises were found to be empty. It appeared the mysterious Mrs Thompson had sold off every item of property and had left the neighbourhood as soon as news of the arrest of her 'husband' had broken.

The next breakthrough came when out of the blue, Mrs Susan Thompson, A.K.A. Susan Grey, turned up at the Greenwich police-house and informed Police-Constable Robinson that, for a consideration, she would provide him with information that could be worth £100. After coming to an agreement with the policeman that she would share in any reward, Mrs Thompson informed Robinson the man he had in custody was, in fact, Charlie Peace, who was wanted for the murder of Mr Arthur Dyson, a civil engineer, in Sheffield, in 1876.

Inspector Phillips, of the Criminal Investigation Department, was quickly dispatched to Sheffield. When the policeman searched the property occupied by the real wife of the prisoner, he uncovered several items recorded as having been stolen during the Blackheath robberies. Mrs Peace denied any knowledge of the London robberies, but she was charged with receiving stolen goods and was remanded in custody.

It was ascertained Mrs Peace had visited her husband in London during the period when the robberies were being committed and had returned to Sheffield with two boxes filled with the proceeds of the crimes. The goods were found hidden in a house in Darnall belonging to Peace.

When applying for a further remand for Mrs Peace, the Chief Constable of Sheffield revealed that, to date, the recovered stolen property had been linked to six separate burglaries in London.

In the meantime, Inspector Phillips had turned his attention to searching the houses of relatives of Peace in the Brightside area of Sheffield and had found a large assortment of items, including sealskin jackets, silk jackets trimmed with fur and lace, slippers, silk stockings and other valuables. They all were believed to have been the proceeds of burglaries and robberies committed by Charlie Peace.

Charles Peace, described as an ex-sailor aged sixty, appeared before Justice Hawkins at the Central Criminal Court on 19 November 1878.

Peace faced trial on charges of 'feloniously shooting at and wounding Edward Robinson, a constable of the Metropolitan Police Force, with intent to resist his lawful apprehension' and 'for a burglary in the dwelling-house of Mr James Alexander Burness, stealing therein a flask and other articles'. Peace pleaded, 'Not Guilty' to both charges.

Messrs Poland and Straight led the prosecution, with Mr Montague Williams and Mr Austin Metcalfe appearing for the defence.

Poland opened for the prosecution by outlining for the jury the events of the night of 10 October, leading to Peace's apprehension in Blackheath. He concluded his opening statement by submitting to the jury there could be no doubt when a man fires five chambers from a revolver loaded with powder and ball at another person, the only motive that could naturally be assumed for such an act was the intention to take the life of that person.

The lawyer then followed up his statement by calling on Police-Constables Robinson and Girling and Police-Sergeant Brown to provide testimony.

Under cross-examination, Robinson said he'd hit the prisoner very hard when he had got possession of the revolver. He claimed not to have heard the prisoner say he had only shot at him to scare him off. The constable finished his testimony by stating he'd had little doubt a burglary was being committed in the house of Mr Burness at the time he had gone into the garden.

Inspector Body was next to provide a statement and he told the Court of his inspection of the property at 2 St John's Park and of finding all the hallmarks of a robbery having been committed.

The case for the prosecution concluded with a statement from house-servant Sarah Cooper, who informed the court that on the morning of the burglary, she had found a bullet lying on the hearth-rug that had corresponded with a hole of similar size in the centre of the dining-room window.

Mr Montague Williams began his statement to the jury, on behalf of the prisoner, by imploring them to leave aside any prejudice that may have been created in their minds by what they may have read about the number of burglaries committed in the neighbourhood. He asked they be guided solely by the evidence relating to the particular charges against the prisoner.

The main basis of the case for the defence, Williams told the jury, was the prisoner had never intended to murder the constable, all he had desired was to escape. Williams argued the facts themselves tended to support that view of the case. If the prisoner really was the desperate man he was reputed to be, having at the time a deadly weapon in his hands, it was almost inconceivable, Williams offered, he could have avoided killing the constable, if he had so intended. The revolver had not been aimed at the chest or stomach of the policeman, but over his head and by his side, to merely frighten him off.

In conclusion, Williams added that he only hoped to relieve the prisoner from what he might call the murderous counts of the indictments, for he would still be responsible to the law on the other charges standing against him.

Justice Hawkins, in summing up, said the case was within a very narrow compass. There was no doubt whatsoever that, on the morning in question, a burglary had been committed at Mr Burness's house and the prisoner had jumped from the window. The constable was, the Judge stated, thus fully justified in apprehending the prisoner on the charge of having committed that burglary.

It was equally clear, the Judge continued, the prisoner had fired five shots from a revolver at the constable. The only question, therefore, was as to the intent with which the shots were fired. If the prisoner had meant only to frighten the policeman, the Judge suggested, he could have done so with a pistol charged only with powder and he had no need to have used powder and ball.

The jury was then asked to retire to consider their verdict. In the blink of an eye, they returned, having found the prisoner guilty of 'feloniously shooting at the constable with intent to murder him'. The jury also complimented Police-Constable Robinson on his bravery in apprehending the prisoner.

Inspector Body then revealed to the court that, in the period since the prisoner had been committed for trial, items relating to a further twenty-six burglaries had been traced back to him.

In passing sentence, Justice Hawkins said the prisoner was, evidently, one of the most accomplished of burglars and one who would not hesitate to commit murder to carry out his end. Declaring he would not be doing his duty if he allowed the prisoner to be at large again, the Judge sentenced Charlie Peace to penal servitude for the rest of his natural life. A spontaneous burst of applause broke out in the courtroom, but matters were quickly brought back under control by the Judge.

When order had been restored, Justice Hawkins called Police-Constable Robinson forward and complimented him on his courageous conduct. The Judge said he would strongly recommend the officer for promotion and declared him to be a man of whom the whole police force could be justifiably proud.

CHAPTER TWO

Mrs Hannah Peace, the wife of Charlie Peace, was brought up on remand at the Sheffield Town Hall, charged with having in her possession goods which were the proceeds of her husband's robberies. At the request of the Chief Constable, the prisoner was remanded for a further week to allow enquiries to continue.

Meanwhile, back in London, the residents of St John's Park, Blackheath, presented Police-Constable Robinson with a handsome watch and chain, together with the not inconsiderable sum for the time of £25, for his bravery in bringing to justice the now notorious burglar, Charlie Peace. Police-Constable Girling and Police-Sergeant Brown each received a reward of £5, for materially assisting in the arrest.

At Hannah Peace's next appearance at Sheffield Town Hall, Inspector Phillips, of the Criminal Investigation Department, Greenwich, spoke as to the large number of robberies committed in the Greenwich and Blackheath areas of London and of his subsequent searches of the prisoner's property in Darnall, near Sheffield. During his visits to Darnall, Phillips had retrieved a large quantity of what he believed to be stolen goods.

The Inspector was asked by Mr Clegg, who was appearing on behalf of the prisoner, if he could confirm whether the prisoner was, or was not, the wife of Charles Peace. Phillips replied he could not swear on the matter, as he had heard statements made on both sides.

Phillips informed the Inquiry it was his belief the prisoner was the owner of the property in Darnall. When he had taken away an ornate clock, the prisoner had claimed it had been brought to her, about five weeks earlier, by another woman, and she had absolutely no idea it might have been stolen.

To strong objections from Mr Clegg, the Inspector, on behalf of the Treasury, asked for the prisoner to be remanded to London. A furious Clegg argued not a shred of evidence had been produced before the Bench to justify them agreeing to such a request. Even assuming the prisoner had been with her husband when the robberies were committed, and he had handed the proceeds over to her, she could not be convicted, as she would be seen to have been acting under his influence.

Clegg characterised the course of action proposed by the policeman to be nothing more than a persecution of his client and, under all the given circumstances, asked the Bench to discharge her immediately.

The Bench was unmoved and Hannah Peace was remanded to appear in London.

During the period the Hannah Peace drama played out, the criminal career of her husband, Charlie, came under intense scrutiny. Not content with having Peace placed in penal servitude for the rest of his natural life, the police re-opened their investigation into the murder of Arthur Dyson in Banner Cross, Sheffield.

The only witness to the murder had been Dyson's wife, who had been so traumatised, and so fearful Peace might come after her, she had left the country to stay with relatives in Cleveland, Ohio, shortly after the murder. With Peace now safely in custody, the Sheffield police were confident they would now be able to persuade Mrs Dyson to return to England to testify against him.

Police-Constable Walsh, who had been assigned the task of providing Mrs Dyson with personal protection before she had left England, was sent to America to track her down and, if possible, induce her to return to give evidence against Peace.

Walsh convinced Mrs Dyson that Peace was no longer able to cause her any harm and, around Christmas 1878, the policeman and his witness set sail from America, bound for Liverpool.

When Hannah Peace finally appeared at the Bow Street Police Court, she stood charged with having been an accomplice in the Blackheath burglaries. Mr Poland and Mr Tickell, instructed by Mr Pollard of the Treasury, conducted the prosecution, Mr Beard appeared on behalf of the prisoner.

Poland began by stating the police had made every possible effort to ascertain the truth of the prisoner's assertion she was the lawful wife of Charles Peace, who had been convicted of burglary and was presently undergoing a penal servitude for life. A thorough search of the records of Somerset House, and of the Parish in Sheffield where the marriage was alleged to have taken place, had been carried out, but no record of such a marriage had been found.

If the prisoner was truly married to Peace, Poland offered, then it was clearly in her own interests to furnish the requisite information to prove the fact, because, as the court was well aware, such proof would materially alter her position in the Inquiry.

The lawyer then referred to the latest edition of 'Russell on Crimes', to show if a wife, in removing property alleged to have been stolen, had acted with the motive of saving her husband from peril, then a charge of a felony could not be sustained against her. In this case, however, it was Poland's view all the known facts led to the conclusion there had been no marriage. The prisoner had, in fact, been living in a house where the man she now claimed to be her husband, was passing himself off as the husband of another woman, named Thompson.

The prisoner herself, Poland continued, had been known as Mrs Ward, and when she had been asked to provide evidence to back up her claim to be married to Charles Peace, she'd been unable to provide any particulars, not even a wedding date, claiming Peace had burned the certificate.

Poland informed the court it was his intention to proceed on the presumption no such marriage had ever occurred and the prisoner's dealings with the stolen property were those of an accomplice in the offences committed. The lawyer then stated he proposed to call witnesses to speak as to the identity of items found in boxes removed by the prisoner from the house of Charles Peace, in Peckham, to the residence of her sister-in-law, in Sheffield.

Numerous witnesses identified a wide range of items laid out in Court. The items included silk pocket-handkerchiefs, night-dresses, slippers, scarves, silk stockings, Indian tablecloths, silver cutlery, silver plate, clocks, watches and many items of jewellery.

Inspectors Phillips and Bonney were then called to provide evidence regarding the discovery of the items produced in Court, before Inspector Pinder Twybell, of the Ipswich Police, was examined.

'On Wednesday 5 November,' Twybell stated, 'I assisted Phillips in a search of the house of Mr William Bolsover, the son-in-law of the prisoner. I, afterwards, returned there and saw the prisoner in the company of Mr Bolsover, Mrs Bolsover and Willie Ward. In the presence of the prisoner, I said to Mr Bolsover, 'We have found a large quantity of property in your house, which we have good reason to believe is stolen. There is a clock here which Inspector Phillips has identified as being part of the proceeds of a burglary in Blackheath. How do you account for it being in your house?' Bolsover replied to me, 'I know nothing about it.' I then said, 'You will have to account for it.' The prisoner then stepped forward and said, 'I brought the clock with me from Hull, about five weeks ago.' I asked her how she had come to be in possession of a clock that had been stolen and she said, 'A tall woman brought it to me, saying a friend had sent it."

'I assisted in a further search on 14 November,' Twybell went on, 'when items were found that had not been there during the search on the 5th. The prisoner claimed to have been married at St George's Church, the year before her daughter, Mrs Bolsover, was born. She said she could not remember the exact date, but stated she had been married, under the name Ward, to Charles Peace. She said her daughter was nineteen years old and told me the witnesses to the marriage were John and Clara Clarke. Both had since died, the prisoner claimed, and Peace had burned the marriage certificate.'

The next witness to be called was Eliza Belfit, who stated, 'On 5 November, I was living in North Street, Nottingham. Mrs Thompson is my sister. I remember her calling at my house at a late hour one night, in October last. She came with the prisoner, whom she introduced as Mrs Ward. Mrs Ward said they had been living together, but they were in some trouble. I told them I had no room to accommodate them and, after a short time, I accompanied them to the railway station.'

'Mrs Ward had placed a large box, oval in shape and very heavy, in the cloakroom,' Belfit continued. 'It took two porters to remove it. Mrs Ward then gave me a ticket for two boxes belonging to Mrs Thompson, who asked me if I'd collect them and take them to my house. Mrs Ward then gave me a small red box, which she said contained a family relic, and asked if I'd look after it for her.'

'About a fortnight later, the prisoner returned and said she would like some items from the red box. She removed something from the box, though I did not see what it was. She then returned the box and asked if I would retain it, together with a sealed parcel she was carrying. I was never made aware of what the box or the parcel contained. Mrs Thompson called on 1 November to collect the boxes belonging to her. I held onto the red box and parcel until 6 November, when Inspector Bonney called.'

With that, Mr Tickell said the case for the prosecution was concluded.

The prisoner, having been asked if she wished to make any statement, said what she'd done had been done by compulsion and she'd had no guilty knowledge any of the items had been stolen. She was then formally committed for trial at the Central Criminal Court.

Hannah Peace, also known as Hannah Ward, appeared before Mr Commissioner Kerr at the 'Old Bailey', on 14 January 1879.

Shortly after the trial had begun, the Commissioner met with Mr Justice Hawkins, a Judge who had been appointed to the Queen's Bench Division, upon a point of law. The Commissioner subsequently informed the jury that Mr Justice Hawkins had concurred with his own view, namely, the charge against the prisoner could not reasonably be supported, as there was sufficient evidence to show the prisoner was married to Charles Peace and, as such, acted under his authority.

Following direction from the Commissioner, the jury declared they were satisfied the prisoner was the wife of Charles Peace. They then recorded a verdict of 'Not Guilty' and the prisoner was formally discharged.

CHAPTER THREE

On 17 January 1879, Charles Peace was charged, before the Sheffield Stipendiary, with the wilful murder of Mr Arthur Dyson, a civil engineer, at Banner Cross on 29 November 1876.

The now notorious Peace drew a sell-out crowd to witness his examination. So great was the crush at the door, a large number of policemen had to be stationed at the entrance to the Sheffield Town Hall to prevent people from forcing entry.

The murder of Arthur Dyson, which had quickly faded from the memory of the public, due to the culprit having never been caught, was now a sensation. Charlie Peace had, in 1876, been living in Darnall and was a neighbour of Dyson. For some reason, the misshapen little man had developed a disturbingly deep affection for his neighbour's wife.

Unsettled by the unwanted attention his wife was receiving from Peace, Dyson had uprooted the family and moved to the other side of town, to take up residence in Banner Cross. Their obsessed neighbour was not about to let the target of his affection slip away so easily and Peace had followed the couple to their new abode.

Determined to speak to Mrs Dyson, away from the protective reach of her husband, Peace had concealed himself in a nearby garden and awaited his prey. As he had lain in wait, he'd seen Mrs Dyson go to a closet at the foot of her garden. When she had returned to the house, Mrs Dyson had been astonished to find herself confronted by her stalker, standing with a revolver in his hand and exclaiming, 'Speak, or I'll fire!'

The terrified woman had let loose a piercing scream that had brought her husband racing to the door. Then the screaming had dissolved, as two thunderous shots had rung out and Arthur Dyson had slumped to the ground, blood seeping from a wound in his head. Two hours later Dyson drew his last breath.

In the meantime, Charlie Peace had taken flight, scaling a wall and racing across an open field, in the direction of Greystones.

A description of the man wanted for the murder of Arthur Dyson had quickly been issued and read as follows:-

'Charles Peace, wanted for murder on the night of the 29 November. He is thin and slightly built, between fifty-five and sixty years of age, five-feet-four-inches tall with grey (almost white) hair, beard and whiskers. He lacks the use of three fingers of his left hand.'

Peace was actually forty-four years old at the time, about five-foot-three in height, though his bow legs made him appear much shorter, and was missing one finger from his left hand. He had cleverly developed a false arm, which could be placed over his own arm to conceal the injury to his hand and make identification more difficult.

Despite the offer of a £100 reward for his apprehension, Peace had quickly gone to ground and his whereabouts were to remain a mystery for the next two years. He had, in fact, eased into a new life in Peckham, London, where he had lived comfortably on the proceeds of an audacious career in burglary, whilst passing himself off as a respectable member of society, with a taste for music and a charitable disposition.

Dressed in prison uniform, Peace took his place in the dock at Sheffield Town Hall at noon. The prosecution was led by Mr Pollard, Mr Clegg appeared on behalf of the prisoner.

Before proceedings had even begun, Mr Clegg applied for an adjournment, on the grounds he had only been instructed that morning, and the prisoner had not known until the previous day he was to be put on trial in Sheffield. The Stipendiary held there to be insufficient grounds for an adjournment and the case proceeded.

Mrs Dyson was the first witness to be examined. 'I am the widow of Arthur Dyson. In 1876 I was living in Darnall with my husband, the prisoner resided next door. The prisoner was a picture framer and he was employed by my husband to frame four pictures.'

'After he had completed the work, the prisoner continued to call at the house. My husband did not welcome the calls and asked the prisoner to cease to visit. This did not seem to deter him and we subsequently moved to Banner Cross, to get away from the unwanted attention.'

'Prior to moving,' the witness continued, 'the prisoner had held a pistol to my head and said if I ignored him he would blow my brains out and then shoot my husband. Consequently, a summons was taken out against the prisoner, but he did not appear and a warrant was issued for his arrest. That was in July.'

'On 29 October 1876, we moved from Darnall to Banner Cross. We had just arrived when I saw the prisoner standing in my garden. He said to me, 'You see, I'm here to annoy you no matter where you go.' I told him there was a warrant out against him, but he merely said he did not give a damn about warrants or the police.'

'I next saw the prisoner on 29 November, at about 8:10pm,' Mrs Dyson continued. 'I was going to the closet in the back yard, at the rear of the house, when I was confronted by the prisoner, who was brandishing a revolver. He said, 'Speak to me, or I'll fire.' I screamed and retreated back into the closet.'

'On hearing my cries, my husband came out of the house. While he was in the passageway, the prisoner fired two shots at him. My husband fell to the ground after the second shot, a bullet having lodged in the second lobe of his brain. He did not speak afterwards and died two hours later inside the house, to which he had been removed. The prisoner, meanwhile, scaled a wall and escaped into a field beyond. I have not seen him since that day, until seeing him here in court this morning.'

At this point, Mr Clegg asked the Stipendiary if he might defer his cross-examination of the witness, observing that, as the prosecution was being conducted on behalf of the Treasury, the matter of expense should not be of any consequence.

Mr Pollard suggested the other evidence in the case should be taken, offering that, if it was, Mr Clegg might find it unnecessary to apply for an adjournment. The decision was made to proceed and the next witness, Mary Ann Gregory, was called.

'I live in Banner Cross Terrace,' Gregory said. 'On the night of the murder, I saw the prisoner crawling under the wall near Mr Dyson's house. Shortly afterwards, I heard the report of a revolver, followed by the screams of Mrs Dyson. I then went out and, on hearing Mr Dyson had been shot, I went into his house and saw him sitting in a chair, with blood streaming from a wound in his head.'

Next up was Sarah Colgreaves. 'I was in the shop owned by Mrs Gregory on the night of Mr Dyson's murder. Earlier that evening, the prisoner had spoken to me, saying he was going to kill the strangers that had come to live in the Terrace. I assumed he meant the Dysons.'

An enraged Peace jumped to his feet and called out, 'This witness has been brought here to tell a parcel of lies.' On being told to retake his seat, Peace said, 'I am on trial for my life and should be allowed to vindicate myself if possible. If you do not wish me to speak you should put a gag in my mouth, because I will always speak up when I hear someone committing perjury against me.'

The Stipendiary asked Peace not to needlessly interrupt the proceedings, but, true to his word, Peace would not be silenced. 'I do not see how it can be possible the witness can positively claim she had any conversation with me. Up until the time she was brought to identify me in Newgate, I had been heavily disguised in such a way as to deceive all the detectives in London.'

After order was restored, the next witness to be called was a labourer, Charles Brassington. 'I was working on the road near Banner Cross on the day of the murder when I was accosted by the prisoner, who asked me, 'Have you noticed any strange people recently coming to live here?' I told him I didn't know of any and he proceeded to show me several photographs and letters, before saying, 'I will make it a warm one for these strangers before morning, I will shoot them both."

Peace could not contain himself and called out, 'Oh, you false man, I said no such thing.'

Brassington concluded his evidence by saying he had next seen the prisoner when he was taken to identify him in Newgate Prison.

The agitated prisoner jumped to his feet again and proclaimed, 'I am not a dog and it should be my right to interrupt the Court when I hear witnesses come forward with convenient statements that are clearly untrue. I have, in my time, witnessed a great deal of injustice in different courts and I would wish to see true justice in this court today. If I am to be hanged, it would only serve to save me from a long, dreary, life of penal servitude, so I do not particularly care about the outcome of the trial. I do, however, demand justice and a fair trial.'

Mr Pollard pointed out that as the prisoner was represented by a solicitor, he had no right to object and the Justice had the power to remove him. The Stipendiary told Pollard he was fully aware of the powers he had, then said he had no wish to use these powers and he wanted to assure the prisoner the Bench had no desire to treat him unjustly.

The case continued, and the next witness was brought forward. 'My name is John Harrison and I am the surgeon called to attend to Mr Dyson after the shooting. When I arrived at the house, I found Mr Dyson lying insensible. He died in his own house two hours after he had been shot. On making a post-mortem examination, I found a bullet had lodged in the left lobe of the brain and this had caused death.'

Some further evidence was then taken as to portraits the prisoner was said to have shown to several of the witnesses, one portrait being of Mrs Dyson, before the case for the prosecution rested.

Mr Clegg's request for an adjournment until the following Wednesday was granted before the prisoner was led away. Large crowds gathered at Sheffield Railway Station to see Charlie Peace depart for London, to return to his cell in Pentonville Prison.

The train journey from Sheffield to London was an uneventful one, but Peace's return journey, for the resumption of his trial, was to prove altogether more interesting.

Irritated by their prisoner's constant requests for trips to the toilet, the two warders accompanying Peace on his train journey north decided to provide him with bags for the purpose of relieving himself. In these less hygiene conscious days, disposal of the urine filled bags was accomplished by throwing them out of the train window.

As the express train raced past Worksop, it was time for the tossing out of a bag. As the bag flew through the open window, it was swiftly followed by something else, the head-first flying figure of the acrobatic prisoner, Charlie Peace. The two open-mouthed warders froze momentarily, but the youngest one reacted quickest and threw out a hand, which managed to latch onto the heel of Peace's boot.

The warder held on grimly as Peace desperately tried to shake him off, kicking out and wriggling to free himself. Despite the battering his bleeding hands were taking from the increasingly frantic escapee, the warder held onto the boot as the train raced on for almost two miles, before he felt the weight lessen considerably and looked down to see the empty boot in his hands. Peace dropped, head first, onto the step-board of the carriage, before bouncing off and rolling onto the rail tracks.

As the struggle had continued, the chief warder, knowing the window was too small to enable him to assist his colleague, had grabbed the communication cord and pulled frantically to signal for the train to stop. The train had travelled for a further mile before the screeching brakes finally took hold and the train shuddered to a halt.

The two warders raced back up the tracks and found Charlie Peace lying where he'd fallen, barely conscious, but still struggling to slip off his manacles. As the warders lifted their prisoner to his feet, the blood began to seep from a wound in his head.

At that time, the slow-train to Sheffield was passing on another line and the warders flagged it down. The three men boarded the train and the warders attended to their prisoner's wounds, as they continued their journey to Sheffield at a more sedate pace.

It had initially, and logically, been thought Charlie Peace had been trying to escape from custody when he'd hurled himself through the open window of the Sheffield bound express train, however, a pencilled note found in his pocket muddied the waters somewhat. The note read, 'Bury me at Darnall. God bless you all. Charlie Peace.'

With evidence now pointing towards a suicide attempt, it became easier to understand why Peace had not waited for the express train to slow down before he'd burst into action. Peace had chosen to take his leap through the window when the train was approaching an area which he had come to love. Although he'd been forced to leave Darnall after the murder of Mr Dyson, his life had been centred there, well as centred as the life of a man like Charlie Peace could be. His daughter and son lived in Darnall and it had been to Darnall his wife had instantly returned after her acquittal.

Apparently, Peace had previously expressed a wish to be buried in the grounds of Darnall Church and if he'd waited a further few minutes before jumping from the train, he would have almost been in sight of the church's tower.

The two Pentonville warders took turns to watch over their prisoner as he made steady improvement under the care of the local police surgeon, Mr Hallam. The normally verbose patient was put on a twenty-four-hour suicide watch, as he retreated into himself.

Sustained by an intake of brandy and milk during the night, Peace instructed his solicitor the following morning, regaining his voice sufficiently to speak against one of the witnesses, whom he believed was perjuring himself.

CHAPTER FOUR

On Friday 24 January 1879, the Sheffield Stipendiary was of the view the Inquiry into the Banner Cross murder could continue, though, given the condition of the prisoner, evidence would be taken in private in the cell corridor at Sheffield Central Police Station.

News of the change of venue was kept from the eager public and, on hearing rumour of the Inquiry resuming, they flocked to the Sheffield Town Hall in their thousands.

Meanwhile, in the relative calm of the Police Station, a table and a few chairs were placed in a second-floor corridor, for the use of officials and the press, before Charlie Peace was carried in by his two trusty warders and placed in a chair at the head of the table.

Peace cut a pathetic figure as he sank into his seat, his head still swathed in bandages. As his eyes darted around, taking in the strange surroundings, he softly moaned, 'Where am I, what's happening here?' On being told they were proceeding with the preliminary Inquiry into the Banner Cross murder, Peace said, 'I shall not be able to stand it, I am so very cold.' The Stipendiary ordered some blankets be brought in.

Mr Clegg, representing the prisoner, said he was ready to hear from the first witness. A weak voice emerged from within the bundle of bandages and blankets at the top of the table, as Peace complained, 'This is not justice. Why is my own solicitor not preventing this and requesting a remand? Mr Clegg, why are you not asking for a remand?'

The Stipendiary made it clear he had no intention of granting a remand and advised Peace to reserve his energy, to enable him to attend to the witnesses as they were called. Mr Clegg then advised his client he would be allowed to say what he wanted during the cross-examination of Mrs Dyson and he should, therefore, save his strength until then.

Mr Pollard, for the prosecution, then rose to say that, after he'd asked a few questions, he proposed to enter into evidence the fact of the prisoner's attempt to escape and his subsequent recapture. On hearing this, Mr Clegg said as soon as any such evidence was produced, he would be requesting a remand. Peace, tired of listening to the legal arguments, said with an air of resignation, 'Oh, never mind, let's just get on with it.'

At last, the first witness, Mrs Dyson, was recalled and examined by Mr Pollard.

'Do you recall the papers and the card produced at the Inquest held relative to the death of your husband in December 1876?' Pollard asked.

'Yes,' the witness replied, 'the card bore the handwriting of my husband, but I could not tell whether the other papers were in his writing.'

The increasingly restless prisoner asked the Inquiry to produce the milkman he'd alleged had delivered notes between himself and Mrs Dyson, but the Stipendiary merely asked him to stop interrupting the witness.

Mrs Dyson then continued. 'Not one of the letters or papers was written on my authority, I have absolutely no knowledge of them.'

'Do you recall ever giving the prisoner a photograph of yourself?' Pollard asked.

'I remember a photograph was taken of myself and the prisoner at the Sheffield Fair in 1876,' Mrs Dyson replied. 'I kept the photograph on my mantelpiece in the kitchen, but it was later taken without my consent and I did not see it again until last week when it was in the hands of the Chief Constable. I also recall another photograph was produced at the Inquest, but that was one that had been removed from my locket. I had noticed the locket was missing from my bedroom and had searched for it, but had been unable to find it.'

Peace, unable to settle, threw his legs up and onto the table in frustration, which brought him yet another rebuke from the Stipendiary.

'Did you tell anyone about this missing locket?' Pollard asked.

'I told my husband and one of the police officers that attended after his murder,' the witness replied.

Continuing with his futile attempts to direct proceedings, Peace asked for the policeman in question to be brought in. Before the Stipendiary could respond, Mr Clegg told his client to be quiet, though this merely resulted in Peace muttering incomprehensibly under his breath.

Having dealt with his client, Mr Clegg turned his attention to the cross-examination of Mrs Dyson and asked about the circumstances under which the photograph from the Sheffield Fair had been taken.

'The photograph was taken during the time I resided in Darnall. At that time, I believed the prisoner to be a respectable man, I had known him for about a year.'

'Did you attend any other fairs with the prisoner?'

'No.'

'Do you recall how long it was between attending the fair in the company of the prisoner and taking out a summons against him for threatening your life?'

'I don't recall the timespan between the two events.'

'Do you recall the date on which you married Mr Dyson?'

'No.'

'You don't remember the date?'

'No.'

'Can you recall what year it was?'

'I can't'.

'Please listen to me,' said an incredulous Clegg, 'do you mean to tell me, upon your oath, you cannot tell me in what year you were married.'

'I cannot, though I could find out.'

'I want to know now,' the indignant lawyer said. 'Do you really mean to stand there and say you don't know the year of your marriage?'

'That's correct, I don't know.'

'Let me ask you a simpler question,' Clegg said, his voice dripping with sarcasm. 'Do you recall where you were married?'

'I was married in Trinity Church, Cleveland, Ohio.'

'Were there any witnesses at this wedding?'

'Certainly.'

'What were their names?'

'My sister, Mrs Thomas Mooney.'

'Her Christian name?'

'Eliza.'

Mr Pollard interjected at this point. 'I really must object to this line of questioning, as to the witnesses who were present.'

'But she says she can't tell the year in which she was married,' the Stipendiary replied.

'I don't wish to interpose, but is there any relevancy? Does the year in which she married have anything to do with the question as to whether her husband was shot?' Pollard asked.

'I don't myself see there is any relevancy, I confess, but in cross-examination, I am content to allow as much leeway as possible,' the Stipendiary replied.

'I thought it my duty to protest,' Pollard said, to which the Stipendiary replied, 'Your objection has been noted, now please let us proceed.'

'I don't wish to spend any longer on this than I can help, but the question was, in what year the witness was married, and I have a good reason for asking full particulars of the facts,' Mr Clegg stated.

'If the witness could have recollected the year in which she was married, I should have considered the matter finished, but as she cannot, I consider the question regarding the witnesses to be necessary,' the Stipendiary proclaimed.

'If she had told me the year, I should have been satisfied,' Clegg said, before turning back to the witness and asking, 'Mrs Mooney was one witness, who was the other?'

'Dr Sergeant,' Mrs Dyson replied.

'Did you get a certificate of your marriage?'

'Certainly.'

'Did you bring the certificate to England with you?'

'No, I left it in the hands of my agents.'

'What are the names of your agents, and where are they located?'

'Barratt and Co. of St Louis, Missouri, USA.'

'Had you any particular objective in leaving your marriage certificate with these agents?'

'I left my papers with the agents because I considered it to be safer than carrying them around with me,' the increasingly agitated witness replied.

Picking up on Mrs Dyson's discomfort, the Stipendiary asked Clegg, 'Is there really any necessity to go into all these particulars?'

'I am bound to say at once, this is a question of credibility as to what actually happened on the day of the shooting,' Clegg stated, 'and as this witness is the only person that can tell us what happened, I think I have the right to test her credibility in every possible way. That is my objective in asking these questions.'

'Of course, there are certain matters which you have the right to go into,' the Stipendiary said, 'but really, as to the marriage, is that necessary?'

'I have a clear objective in questioning her fully about the marriage, in consequence of what I have been instructed she has previously told someone else about it,' Clegg teased.

'Very well, you may continue.'

Turning his attention back to the witness, Clegg asked, 'Was your husband friendly with the prisoner?'

'Yes, at first.'

'Did the prisoner frame any pictures for you?'

'Yes.'

'Can you tell me what they were?'

'Yes,' the increasing monosyllabic witness replied.

'Please tell me.'

'There was a portrait of my sister and one of Mr Dyson, my brother and my little boy.'

'Anybody else?'

'There was another one.'

'What was it?'

'There were two taken from Harper's Weekly.'

'Was one of them a portrait of your husband's mother?' Clegg asked, attempting to quicken the pace.

'Yes, there was a portrait of my husband's mother.'

'Will you tell me when Peace framed the picture of your husband's mother?'

'He did not frame that picture. That one was in a pot frame, which I bought, the ones he did were in gilt frames.'

His patience again sorely tested, Mr Pollard tried to intervene. 'I really must make an objection to all this, I shall leave it to you, Sir.'

The Stipendiary nodded and asked Clegg whether he really needed to go further into what appeared to be extraneous matters.

'If you want me to do so,' Clegg said, 'I shall tell you what my objective is, but I do not want the witness to hear. I have an objective in view and it is a material objective, a most material objective.'

'Supposing she gives the answers as to the pictures,' the Stipendiary said, 'that, of itself, is not, to my idea, of sufficient importance to go further with the matter.'

'It is much more important than that,' Clegg offered.

The Stipendiary shrugged, then said, 'Very well, but if your objective is merely a question of general credibility, then I consider it is going too far.'

Unperturbed, Clegg pressed on. 'Did you ever ask the prisoner to frame the portrait of your husband's mother?'

'Yes,' Mrs Dyson replied, 'but he never got around to doing it.'

'Did you ever write him any letters about it?'

'No.'

At that point, Clegg reached over to the table and picked up a batch of letters, before passing one, marked 'No.6', to the prisoner and asking, 'Is that letter in your handwriting?'

'No.'

'Is it in your husband's handwriting?'

'No.'

'Do you recognise the handwriting?'

'No.'

'Did any other person know of your wish for the prisoner to frame the portrait of your husband's mother, besides you, him and your husband?'

'Not that I'm aware of.'

'Have you ever seen the prisoner write?'

'No.'

'Are you willing to swear you have never seen the prisoner write?'

'I never saw him write, as far as I can recall. I saw him getting my husband to write letters and receipts on his behalf. I did not actually see him write, though I saw him sitting at the writing table, with writing materials before him.'

'Would you be able to recognise his writing if you saw it?'

'No, I don't even know if he could write, because he used to come and get Mr Dyson to write for him.'

'Will you please now listen as I read this letter,' Clegg said.

'Is that the letter marked 'No.6'?' the Stipendiary asked.

'Yes,' the Clerk of Court replied.

The witness was then passed the letter to peruse, as Clegg read out what was contained in it.

The letter read as follows:-

'Saturday afternoon,

I write you these few lines to thank you for all your kindness, which I shall never forget, from you and your wife. She is a good one. Does she know you are to give me the things or not? How can you keep them concealed? One thing I wish you to do is to frame his mother's portrait and send it with my music book.

If you please, do it when he is in. Many thanks for your kind advice, I hope I shall benefit from it. I shall try to do right by everyone if I can and shall always look upon you as friends.

Goodbye. I have not much time. Burn this when you have read it.'

'Now madam,' Clegg sneered, 'will you venture to swear this document is not in your handwriting?'

'No, it is not my writing,' Mrs Dyson replied.

As if he had just awoken from a slumber, Peace stirred to release an audible groan, before murmuring under his breath about the injustice of the Inquiry.

Ignoring the interruption, Clegg continued to question Mrs Dyson. 'Now, Madam, remember you are on your oath.'

'I remember.'

'You were very intimate with the prisoner were you not?'

'Yes.'

'Have not you and the prisoner, without your husband or the prisoner's wife, been to a place of amusement?'

'I have been with him and his wife and daughter.'

'That is not what I asked you,' Clegg snapped, 'I asked if you have been with him alone to places of amusement.'

'Not to places of amusement, I have called at one place in Sheffield with him alone.'

'What place?'

'I do not know where it is. The prisoner said there was a man there he knew and he called him his brother.'

'What sort of place was this?'

'It was a public-house,'

'Do you know which street it was in?'

'No.'

'Have you been to the theatre with the prisoner?'

'Yes, I have been with him and his wife and daughter.'

'Was your husband there?'

'No, I had other friends along with me.'

'Have you been to the Albert Hall alone with the prisoner?'

'No, I was never alone with him at the Albert Hall, his daughter was with him.'

Peace again emerged from his cocoon of bandages and blankets and, leaning towards the table, said, in a feeble voice, 'Send for Mr Cowan.'

'Will you please be quiet,' Clegg pleaded, before turning back to the witness and asking, 'Have you been with the prisoner in any other public-houses?'

'No, not along with him. He has followed me into public-houses when my husband and I were together.'

'He has followed you into public-houses?'

'Yes.'

'What public-house has he followed you into?'

'One in Darnall, there were one or two of them, I can't remember the names.'

'Was one the Duke of York? Did you not go there alone?'

'No, I used to go there with my husband.'

'Did you ever go to a public-house, get something to drink and tell the landlord to put it down to Peace, the prisoner?'

'No, I once had a soda-water in a public-house with the prisoner, but that is all.'

Moving on, Clegg asked, 'Had you any quarrel with the prisoner?'

'Yes, he was a nuisance, running after me all the time.'

'Before you took out a summons against him, had you had any actual quarrel with the prisoner?'

'Not a quarrel as such, it's just he was such a nuisance about the house, that's what made me do it.'

It was time for another interruption from Peace and, as he lay his head on his hands at the table, he murmured, 'Let me go away now, let me lie down, I cannot bear it anymore.'

Mr Hallam, the police surgeon who was present in Court, walked up to the prisoner and took his pulse. Mr Clegg suggested Peace be allowed to put his feet up on a chair to make himself more comfortable. Mr Hallam then offered, 'That seems reasonable, he would be just as well being here as in his cell.'

'Very well then, we can proceed,' the Stipendiary declared.

Clegg resumed his lengthy cross-examination.

'Had you had any unpleasantness before you went to Mansfield?'

'He was a constant source of annoyance, by his disagreeableness and his jumping over the wall and listening at the door all the time.'

'He did what?'

'He listened at the door and was very disagreeable indeed.'

The questions and answers continued to flow.

'By what train did you go to Mansfield?'

'The afternoon train.'

'Did you go together to Mansfield?'

'No, he followed us.'

'Were you together in Mansfield?'

'He came into the house where we were having tea and sat down.'

'Do you know a person named Kirkham, a milkman who used to deliver milk to you?'

'Yes, I know the milkman, or I should know him if I saw him.'

Kirkham was then brought forward and the witness confirmed she recognised him, though she had not been aware of his name until now.

'Now then,' Clegg said, 'have you ever given him notes, with instructions to pass them to Peace?'

'I gave him two receipts to pass on that Mr Dyson had written, for pictures the prisoner had framed,' the witness replied

'Were they within an envelope?'

'No, they were not in an envelope.'

'Have you not passed on notes or little scraps of paper?'

'No notes or scraps, only receipts.'

'Where did your husband keep his address cards?' Clegg asked, opening up a fresh line of questions.

'In his writing-desk.'

'Locked up?'

'No.'

'Where was the writing-desk located?'

'In the sitting-room.'

'Did you have any address cards?'

'No.'

'Did you ever use any of your husband's?'

'No.'

As the flicker of a smirk passed over his face, Clegg pressed on. 'The prisoner had a daughter named Jane, is that correct?'

'Yes, Jane Ann.'

Handing an address card to the witness, the lawyer said, 'Please look at that card, which is in the same handwriting as the other papers, and read out what it says.'

'I cannot read it, as the writing is not clear to me.'

'Let me assist you then, you can read and write I assume?' Clegg asked, with more than a hint of sarcasm.

'Yes, I can read and write.'

'Now this is what it says: 'He is going out later. I won't go if I can help it. Come see me. Love to Janey.' Will you venture to swear you did not write that message.'

'I did not write that,' the defiant witness replied.

'Has this address card been altered from Mr to Mrs?'

'I cannot tell.'

'Look at it closely.'

'Yes, a letter 's' has been added, though it was certainly not added by me.'

Moving on, Clegg asked, 'Did you know a little girl named Hutton?'

'I don't recall that name,' Mrs Dyson replied.

'Do you know Mrs Hutton, who lives in Britannia Road?'

'I don't recall the name. I may know her if I saw her, but I can't tell her by name.'

'Did you ever meet the prisoner at Mrs Hutton's house?'

'No, I never met him there.'

'Were you and he never together at Mrs Hutton's?'

'He came in there one day when I was present, I had gone to get the girl to run an errand for me.'

'Mrs Hutton's little girl?' the Stipendiary asked.

'A little girl who lived down the hill,' the witness answered, somewhat evasively.

'Did you know what her name was?'

'That must have been her name, Hutton.'

'Did you give notes to this little girl, Hutton, to pass to the prisoner?' Clegg asked.

'No, I never did so.'

Clegg then requested a pen and paper be passed to the witness, before saying, 'Will you please write out the following for me: 'I will write you a note when I can, perhaps tomorrow."

Mr Clegg looked at the freshly written note, before comparing it with a note that had been lodged as evidence. He then asked the witness to finish the note by copying the remainder of the original note, which read: 'You can give me something as a keepsake if you like, but I don't want to be covetous and take them from your wife and daughter.'

Clegg then compared the notes again and said, 'You have not written the second half nearly as well as you wrote the first half.'

'That's the best I can do,' Mrs Dyson stated firmly.

'Look at the first line on the card I read out to you,' Clegg requested, 'do you still swear that is not your handwriting?'

'I say that is not my writing.'

Clegg asked the witness a further four times to swear on her oath the card was not in her writing, each time receiving the same reply.

'She will only use the word 'say' in her response, I want her to say, 'I swear',' the lawyer pleaded, after being asked by the Stipendiary how many times he was going to repeat the question.

'She has already been sworn in,' Mr Pollard interjected.

'She is on her oath, certainly,' Clegg admitted before the exchange was ended by a call from the prisoner, 'Make her swear.'

The next phase of questions followed this now familiar pattern. Clegg would establish facts that could only have been known to the witness and the prisoner, then draw, from the bundle of notes held in evidence, a letter or card referring directly to these facts. Each time, the witness would claim the notes were not in her handwriting.

Eventually, the Stipendiary had heard the line of questioning once too often, remarking to Clegg, 'You have got quite as much to damage her credibility as will be sufficient for you, you must reserve this cross-examination for the trial.'

Clegg contended it was important he be allowed to proceed as he wished and said he intended to persist in asking these questions until he was stopped.

'Then I stop you now,' the Stipendiary snapped, 'you have proven quite enough to indict her for perjury, for that is all it can lead to. You can indict her for perjury if she has spoken falsely.'

'You can do more than that,' piped up the prisoner, before he was fed medication that led to him whining, 'I can't swallow it.'

After Peace had settled down again, Clegg resumed his cross-examination.

In answer to the barrage of questions that followed, Mrs Dyson claimed; she had never given the prisoner an American cent; she had never borrowed any money from the prisoner; she had a son named William; she was not aware of the prisoner having given her son any coppers; she had left Darnall because the prisoner had annoyed her and she and her husband were afraid of the prisoner.

Having been told by neighbours the prisoner used to visit Darnall at night dressed in female attire, Mrs Dyson claimed she and her husband were terrified Peace intended to come for them in the night.

'Have you ever received letters from the prisoner,' Clegg asked.

'No, oh yes, I have received threatening letters from him. Mr Chambers has them,' the witness replied.

'What were you doing on the night of the murder?'

'Before going to the closet, I'd just put my son to bed,'

'Did you see Peace through the bedroom window?'

'No, I first saw him when I was coming out of the closet.'

'When you saw him, did you say to him, 'You old devil, what are you doing here now? I should have thought you had brought enough disgrace upon me.'?'

'No, I do not recall saying anything to him. He said to me, 'Speak, or I'll fire.'"

'Do you recall the prisoner saying, 'I have come to try and see you and get your husband to come to terms, as I am away from my wife.'?'

'No, I did not speak with him.'

In reply to Clegg's final burst of questions, Mrs Dyson stated; when her husband came up, the prisoner was by the side of the closet; her husband did not speak to either herself or the prisoner; her husband and Peace were never out of her sight; her husband did not try to get hold of the prisoner, he was not close enough; she did not hear Peace say, 'If you don't stop I'll fire'; there was no struggle between the two men; she was only a few feet away when her husband was shot and she had thrown her lantern down when she'd seen her husband fall, but she'd had it in her hand until then.

Mrs Dyson was then re-examined by Mr Pollard. Her husband, she said, had not taken any steps forward after the bullet had struck him, he'd dropped instantly. Mrs Dyson then clarified she had received the threatening letters when she'd been living in Darnall. There had been two letters, perhaps more, and she'd given them to her husband, who had, in turn, passed them to his solicitor.

With that, the epic examination of Mrs Dyson was concluded.

After hearing from Police-Constable Pearson, who had been involved in the unsuccessful attempts to locate Charlie Peace after the murder of Arthur Dyson, the court was informed by Mr Pollard he next intended to call evidence as to the recent escape and recapture of the prisoner, on the grounds that if

Peace had been an innocent man he would not have tried to get away.

Mr Clegg immediately objected and the Stipendiary, pointing out that at the time of the escape attempt Peace was already a convict under a sentence of penal servitude for life, said if Pollard did call any such evidence, he would not admit it on the depositions. The matter was subsequently dropped and the case for the prosecution was concluded.

Mrs Dyson's depositions were read back to her before she signed them, then the depositions of the witnesses taken at the previous hearing were read over, before being formally signed.

The Stipendiary then informed the prisoner of the charges against him and cautioned him, before asking if he had anything he wished to say.

A noticeably nervous Mr Clegg quietly advised his client, 'If you take my advice, you will simply say you are 'not guilty'.'

'I am not guilty,' Peace said, but he just couldn't let it lie at that, adding, 'and I must say I have not had justice done me in proving I am not guilty. That's what I want, I want justice done me. Why have my witnesses not been called? Can my witnesses be called upon at my trial if I cannot afford to pay their expenses?'

'What exactly is it you are complaining about?' the startled Stipendiary asked.

'I want my witnesses to be called to prove I have really not done this,' Peace replied.

'Are the witnesses to be called here? You must ask your solicitor whether he proposes to call them or not.'

'I say I am not guilty, and I say I have not had justice done me to prove I am not guilty. There are witnesses, and I say I can prove this base, bad woman threatened her husband's life and her own life. I cannot talk anymore on the matter now, I am feeling too ill.'

'Please listen, and hear what has been written as your statement,' the Stipendiary said, 'it is this: "I say I am not guilty, have not had justice done to me and want my witnesses to be called."'

'That's it,' Peace replied, 'and I say I can prove she has threatened his life and her own life and she carried a pistol.'

'You are not taking your trial today, this is only a preliminary Inquiry,' the Stipendiary said, before turning to Mr Clegg and asking, 'Are there any witnesses or not?'

'I do not intend calling any today,' Clegg replied. His answer was greeted by a snarling request from his client, 'I want to speak to you before you go.'

The Stipendiary then asked Peace if he would put his signature to the statement. 'I will try,' Peace said. As he rose unsteadily to his feet, one of the warders tried to assist him, only to be met by a petulant response. 'Do not touch me. Let me be.'

Having made his weary way to the document, Peace started to sign his name, before declaring, 'I cannot see, I have no spectacles.' Despite the visual impairment, Peace finally managed to put something resembling a signature to the statement.

'You are committed to taking your trial on this charge at the assizes at Leeds,' the Stipendiary declared.

'When are they?' Peace asked.

'They will begin the very next week.'
Peace was then removed to his cell, where he entered into a lengthy discussion with his solicitor.

CHAPTER FIVE

Details were beginning to emerge of the evasive actions Charlie Peace had employed following the Banner Cross murder, as he had made little secret of them among those who knew him well.

To a group of friends, he had said, 'Do you want to know how I managed to dodge the police?'

'Of course,' his eager listeners had replied.

'Then I shall show you.'

Peace had then asked the group to turn their backs to him for a moment. When the men were asked to turn around again, a look of astonishment had spread across their faces. Standing before them was a man with a protruding chin and curled lips. The contortion of the man's features had forced the blood to rush into his face, leaving him with the appearance of what was termed at the time, a Mulatto.

One of the wide-eyed spectators finally found his voice and had said, 'No wonder you could get clear from Sheffield when you can change your face like that.'

Peace had simply laughed and had boasted, 'I can do some dodges. I can dodge any detective in existence. I did not change my face much when I left Sheffield, but I will tell you about it.'

'After what happened at Banner Cross,' Peace had continued, 'I ran across some fields, in the direction of the Endecliffe Hall, to Crookes and Sandygate and then back down to Broomhill, where I took a cab and rode down to the church gates. There, I got out and went to the house of a relative, where I changed clothes.'

The story had continued. 'I, afterwards, went to Rotherham, then bought a train ticket for Beverley. I left the train at Normanton and, retaining the ticket, took another one to York. I stayed a night or two in York, before going on to Beverley and from there to Hull.'

Peace had then told the enthralled group how he had eked out an existence by committing a series of robberies in Hull, before staying for short spells in Leeds, Bradford and Manchester. From Manchester, he had moved on to Nottingham and it was there he had met the now notorious Mrs Thompson.

He had not been long in Nottingham before he had committed an audacious robbery of silk, which had netted the huge sum, for the time, of £300. The highly skilled thief had been staying at a lodging-house with Mrs Thompson when, one night, they'd been disturbed by a policeman.

Peace had then taken up the story of what had happened next for his captivated crowd. 'The officer wanted to know who I was and where I came from. I told him I was a hawker. The officer demanded to see my licence and asked what goods I was carrying. I told him both the licence and goods were kept downstairs and asked him to go down and wait, to allow my wife and me to get dressed.'

'As soon as he had gone out the door,' Peace had continued, 'I jumped out of the window and ran off. I took shelter in a nearby lodging-house and, when sufficient time had passed, I sent the landlady back to my former lodgings to collect my boots. With

Nottingham becoming too hot for me, I moved back to Sheffield, where I did a good bit of work.'

'One of the places I robbed, was a house at the corner of Havelock Square. I did very well there, but I saw a 'bobby' coming and had to scarper quick-style. I was still in Sheffield at the time the Inquest was being held into the death of Mr Dyson. I then went to Hull, to see my wife and give her some money, before travelling on to London with Mrs Thompson.'

The saga had continued. 'On two occasions while I was in London, I met Bill Fisher, a man with whom I had previously worked. The first time I met him was on the Holborn Viaduct and, as I passed him, I heard him say, 'Why, that's Charlie Peace.' I got myself lost in the crowds immediately, but not long afterwards I bumped into him again, on the steps leading into Farringdon Street. On that occasion, our eyes met again and I was forced to get out of there sharpish. Those were the only two times I was worried about being recognised. I have often met the best London detectives and stared them straight in the face, but they have never recognised me.'

Bill Fisher, on his return to Sheffield, had, in fact, informed the police of his chance encounters with Peace and the Sheffield Police had subsequently notified their colleagues in London the wanted criminal was living in their midst.

Peace was not the only one to open up about his escapades. The once mysterious Mrs Thompson decided to cash in on her fifteen minutes of fame and sold her story to the press.

Thompson, whose maiden name had been Susan Grey, first made Peace's acquaintance in Nottingham, whilst he was engaged in an extensive bout of burglaries, the proceeds of which he had brought back to his house. Silver plates, timepieces and perishable goods were stolen in large quantities.

The burglar had varied his operations by making frequent trips to Hull, where he had committed further burglaries. During one such sojourn, he had found it necessary to 'fire wide' at a policeman who had nearly captured him.

Although she had been fully aware Peace made his living from the proceeds of his crimes, Mrs Thompson maintained she had never received any of the items he'd stolen and claimed any dresses she had been given had been legitimately bought by Peace.

One of Peace's most ambitious robberies during that period had been the 'great cloth robbery' he'd carried out at a factory in Nottingham in June 1877. As he had been making his escape through a wood-yard, he'd been confronted by a night-watchman. The diminutive burglar had somehow managed to leave the man so terrified he had later refused to provide the police with any meaningful description of his assailant.

Peace had managed to stay under the radar during his Nottingham crime spree until his 'great silk robbery' attracted so much attention a reward of £50 was offered for information leading to the arrest of the perpetrator.

Acting on information they had received, the police had arrived one night at the house where Mrs Thompson, known at the time as Mrs Bailey, and Peace were staying. The detectives had found the couple in bed and had made the mistake of going downstairs to allow them to get dressed.

Peace had dressed quickly and then made his escape through the bedroom window, squeezing himself between two iron bars barely seven inches apart. Whilst the detectives had waited patiently downstairs, Peace had made his way to the banks of the River Trent and had taken lodgings in a public-house on the riverside.

As soon as he could, Peace had sent word to Mrs Thompson to join him, which she had duly done, and the couple had then fled to London.

After settling in the Lambeth District of London, Peace had embarked on his greatest crime spree yet, making him the most notorious burglar in the country. Often carrying out five or six robberies a night, Peace would return with valuable plunder reflecting the increasingly lucrative targets he had found among the London elite.

Mrs Thompson, tired of living in apartments, had asked Peace to provide her with a proper house and he had agreed to do so. He had, at that time, just committed a particularly fruitful robbery and Mrs Thompson was dispatched to Hull to pass some of the proceeds to his wife, Hannah.

On her return, Peace had asked Mrs Thompson if it would be acceptable for his wife and son to come and live with them. Mrs Thompson had agreed to the unusual arrangement and Hannah Peace and her son Willie had soon arrived in the big city. Shortly afterwards, the group had moved to Greenwich and taken two adjoining houses there, Peace and Mrs Thompson living in one and Hannah and the boy in the other.

Following his success in London, Peace had taken his show on the road, committing a series of robberies in the provinces. One raid in Southampton had netted £50 in gold, silver and Bank of England notes. Peace had decided to use the takings from this robbery to invest in the purchase of a pony and trap, to make it easier to transport his stolen goods from the outlying areas.

Peace would regularly take the tram or train to the targets he had marked for robbery, with arrangements being made for the pony and trap to be driven out to meet up with him at an appointed hour.

Many of the stolen items had been sold on through Jewish traders, who were faced with the threat that if Peace was ever captured due to being given up by any of them, he would confess all to the police and inform on all his accomplices.

Mrs Thompson revealed Peace, when on a job, always carried a revolver, a jemmy, a sharp knife and various sized screws (to secure the rooms he entered so he would not be disturbed). He would never use a skeleton key, as he was capable of removing a panel or pane of glass quickly and silently. His trousers, in addition to ordinary pockets, were fitted at the rear with special pockets, to carry his revolver and housebreaking tools.

Peace would also carry with him a burglar's stick and a portable ladder with seventeen steps, which he could fold into a particularly compact form. The ladder was fitted with hooks, for fastening it to walls and window ledges, but it was rare for the agile little thief to have to make use of it.

The burglar had owned four revolvers, one of which was always left in the possession of Mrs Thompson, so she could defend herself if necessary. When Peace was finally arrested, Mrs Thompson had destroyed the three pistols that had been left in the house and the money and furniture had been split between Hannah Peace and herself.

On the morning after his final appearance before the Sheffield Stipendiary, Charlie Peace was examined by the police surgeon, Mr Hallam, who certified the prisoner was in a condition that would allow him to be transported from his cell at the Central Police Station to Wakefield, where he would remain in the county prison until his trial at the Leeds Assizes.

The authorities were keen to carry out the transfer away from the glare of the public, but the legend of Charlie Peace was, by now, a runaway train and the daily feeding of information from the press had simply made the public hungry for more.

As soon as the prison van horses were seen in Castle Green, the thoroughfare leading to the cells, suspicions were aroused that Peace was being moved and a large crowd soon gathered outside the police station. Immediately after the horses had been led through the archway of the parade ground, the gates were closed and a number of policemen were put in place to quell the press of the crowd.

After the horses were attached to the prison van, Peace was carried from his cell by the two Pentonville warders and placed in the vehicle, which was furnished with a mattress and several rugs. The master criminal cut a sad and pathetic figure, his features pale and haggard and his head still swathed in bandages.

The warders and several police officers got into the back of the van to guard their prisoner, but they saw no need to shackle him. The gates of the prison yard were then thrown open and the van, behind which rode four mounted police officers, made its way rapidly towards the railway station.

An even larger crowd had anticipated Peace's arrival at the station, but, rather than stopping at the passenger entrance, the prison van was driven into a siding, far beyond the ticket office.

The crowd were, however, not going to be denied and they pushed past policemen and railway officials and swarmed down the line towards the train. They arrived just in time to see Peace being carried from the prison van into a guards van that had been placed in the siding to convey him to Wakefield. People tried to climb up to catch a glimpse of the infamous prisoner, but they were eventually pushed back.

Finally, the London to Leeds train arrived and the guard's van conveying the convict was run out of the siding and coupled to it. The train slowly pulled away from the station, leaving the crazed crowd behind.

CHAPTER SIX

The public hunger for information on the exploits of Charlie Peace showed no sign of abating, so the newspapers did their best to feed it and Mrs Thompson did her best to help them fill their column inches. She provided a fresh statement, which read as follows:-

'He told me he was born in Angel Street, Sheffield, of respectable parents. The published accounts of his age are wrong, he is not fifty years of age or anything like it, but the life he has led had made him look older.

His father was a caretaker of the animals in Wombwell's Menagerie and used to travel the country with the show, his wife and children accompanying him on occasions. Peace was eleven years old when his father died, leaving him to look out for himself. His first depredation was at a fair in Sheffield, where he robbed a gentleman of his watch.

At this time, he was working at a button factory and living with his mother. For three years afterwards, he continued his depredations in Sheffield. He told me he always worked alone, even at that time. On one occasion, he broke into a house at night and abstracted a gold watch and chain from a bedroom where persons were asleep.

I cannot say why he left Sheffield, but the next place he went to was Bradford, leaving his mother behind. He knew something about carving and gilding, I do not know where he learned it but he was always proud of it and he obtained employment in that line of business in Bradford.

Of course, this work did not interfere with his usual depredations, it was merely a blind. There was a 'miscellaneous' shop in Bradford where he used to dispose of his takings. During that period, he always had plenty of money and could command from £50 to £80. He boasted he sometimes carried out three or four robberies a night in Bradford, where he stayed for two years, making that town his headquarters.

On one job, he fired at a policeman and, in consequence, a £50 reward was offered for his apprehension. A description of him was published and his name was given as Charles Frederick Peace. He went back to Sheffield for a time, where his mother was still living. He used to go into the countryside around Sheffield, breaking into gentlemen's houses chiefly. Sometimes he would go longer distances and it was on one of these excursions he first met Hannah.

From Sheffield, he moved to Leeds, remaining there for three weeks, passing himself off as a one-armed man. He made a successful raid there, obtaining watches, jewels and rings, which he was able to get rid of in Sheffield.

Generally, he would stay at coffee-houses when he went to a strange place, doing his business in a two-hour period and always getting back before midnight. That was why he was never suspected by any of the coffee-house keepers.

He always carried a jemmy, about fourteen inches long with a screw at one end, and a chisel, which could also be used as a plane, at the other. The screw end of the jemmy was for use when the chisel end could not get purchase in a door.

Whilst in Leeds, he committed a robbery of ostrich feathers and in consequence of a reward of £100 being offered for his apprehension, he returned to Sheffield and lived for a spell with Hannah, who was going under the name Mrs Ward at that time.

Moving on to Bristol, he remained there for three weeks, disguised as the one-armed man. He did very well there and made a great haul of jewellery from a raid on a private villa in Clifton.

Having fenced his booty, he took up residence in Hull and stayed there for six months, until he broke into a public-house, where he almost got caught as he was making off with cigars and some money.

From Hull, he made an excursion to York, where he stayed for nearly a month, robbing mansions and disposing of the proceeds to pawnbrokers who were known to be receivers of stolen property.

Next, he went to Manchester, where he and Mrs Ward took a bar, shop and eating-house at Bank Top. When at the shop one day, he was recognised by a man who had been imprisoned with him once for burglary.

Around that time, a young policeman on his rounds found a parcel of stolen property in a drainpipe and took it back to the police station. He was told to take it back to where he'd found it and the location was staked-out by the police. When Peace came to collect the parcel, he was apprehended. He tried to resist the officers and was treated so roughly by them that a gentleman followed to complain about their conduct at the police station. After finding out who the prisoner was, the gentleman withdrew his complaint.

While in prison awaiting trial, he wrote a letter, which led the police to search the eating house in Manchester, where they found a cache of stolen books and pictures.

He was caught trying to escape from prison by means of a rope, before being tried and sentenced to seven years of penal servitude. This was his first big sentence. I believe that, at different times, altogether he has received twenty-one years of penal servitude, but in some cases, his very good conduct reduced his terms.

In the intervals between his convictions, he visited Liverpool, where he did very good business but had to leave when he became 'wanted'. Utilising various disguises, he also spent time in Birmingham, Hull and Bradford, before settling down again in Sheffield.

The first thing he did in Sheffield was open a carver and guilder's shop, but the shop failed and he and Mrs Ward relocated to Darnall. There, Peace met a clergyman who, as a chaplain, had known him in prison. The clergyman told Peace he would not reveal anything about his past, provided he conducted himself properly. Peace promised he would lead an amended life, but a few weeks later he robbed the clergyman's house.

It was about this time he first met Mrs Dyson. After the Dyson affair, he went to Bristol and from there back to Sheffield. He was in town at the time of the Inquest.'

Mrs Thompson finished by saying she believed Peace to be very hopeful as to the result of his defence.

Charlie Peace appeared at the Leeds Assizes, before Mr Justice Lopez, on 4 February 1879, charged with the murder of Arthur Dyson at Banner Cross, near Sheffield, on 29 November 1876.

Mr Campbell Foster Q.C. and Mr Shield led the prosecution, with Mr Lockwood and Mr Wortley acting for the defence.

Foster opened the case for the Crown by admitting he could not disguise the fact the case that was about to commence had been so much commented on by the press and the public, it would be a difficult matter for the jury to enter upon the trial as though the matter was for the first time being brought before them.

It was, however, Foster stated, his duty to call upon the jury to reject all preconceived ideas as to the case and to try the prisoner, simply and fairly, upon the sworn testimony presented before them, without reference to any other information or belief they might have as to the prisoner, or his life.

The Q.C. then moved on to outline the facts of the case, detailing the history of the acquaintance of Mr and Mrs Dyson with Peace.

The first witness to be called was a surveyor, Mr Johnson of Sheffield. He spoke as to the accuracy of a plan of Dyson's house in Banner Cross that had been entered as evidence.

Under cross-examination by Mr Lockwood, Johnson said he had known Mr Dyson personally and described him as a tall, muscular man, though perhaps a little delicate in health. Johnson added Dyson was a civil engineer and about six-foot-six-inches in height.

Next up was Catherine Dyson, who was examined by Mr Shield. Mrs Dyson went through the now familiar background to Peace's acquaintance with herself and her husband, before a card was produced in court, in the handwriting of Mr Dyson, which read: 'Charles Peace is requested not to interfere with my family.' After the writing of the card, Peace had no longer been admitted into the family's house, but he had remained a continual source of annoyance, regularly loitering close to the property.

On one occasion, Mrs Dyson recalled, Peace had bumped into her husband on the street and had tried to trip him up. That same evening, she had been talking to some neighbours when Peace had approached her and pointed a revolver at her face. This had occurred in front of her house in Darnall, in the presence of four witnesses. Peace had then threatened he would blow her husband's brains out too, before stating he was carrying 'death for six' if anyone tried to interfere with him.

Mrs Dyson then recounted the details of her family's flight to Banner Cross, the summons taken out against Peace and the dreadful events leading up to the murder of her husband.

Before Mr Lockwood began his cross-examination, he warned Mrs Dyson it may take some time and offered her the opportunity to be seated. Mrs Dyson declined the offer.

In answer to the questions put to her by Lockwood, Mrs Dyson provided the following responses:-

She had left her husband reading when she went to the outhouse.

She'd had to pass through the room where he was sitting to go outside.

When she'd first heard Peace, she had been just coming out of the outhouse.

The passage was about three feet wide and she'd seen all that passed very distinctly.

Her husband had moved towards Peace at walking pace.

Her husband had never touched Peace (though, on being pressed, she would not swear he had not attempted to touch him).

Her husband had fallen on his back.

Peace had not struck her husband in the face with his fist.

Lockwood then moved on to question Mrs Dyson about her relationship with Peace, before producing a batch of letters which he passed to her. As she had done when appearing before the Stipendiary, Mrs Dyson denied any knowledge of the letters and claimed they were not in her handwriting.

The lawyer then turned his attention to a ring Peace had given to Mrs Dyson. The witness's memory fogged over at this stage and she was unable to recall when it was given to her or whether she had shown it to her husband or not. What she did recall was the ring had been too small for her and she had thrown it away, as she had not considered it to be worth keeping.

The remainder of the cross-examination closely followed the line of questioning that had taken place during the Inquiry, with Mrs Dyson resolutely sticking to her guns regarding any inappropriate intimacy with Peace and denying the passing of notes to him through intermediaries. With that, the cross-examination was concluded.

Mary Ann Gregory, the wife of grocer John Gregory, was the next witness to be called. Examined by Mr Foster, Mrs Gregory provided her statement. 'The house where I live is next door to the one formerly occupied by Mr and Mrs Dyson. They came to live there at the end of October 1876, and on the night they arrived, the prisoner came into our shop.'

'I called my husband into the shop,' Mrs Gregory continued, 'and he and the prisoner conversed together for about ten minutes. I was out of the shop for part of the time and I cannot tell what the conversation was about. The prisoner bought half an ounce of tobacco and, during the time I was in the shop, I had a good look at him.'

Mrs Gregory went on. 'I next saw the prisoner on 29 November 1876. At about 7pm, I saw him in the passage of our house and he asked me if my husband was at home. I told him my husband was not at home and he went away. About five or ten minutes afterwards, I looked out of the door again.'

'Had you heard any noise at all?' Foster asked.

'No, none.'

'Did you see anybody?'

'Yes, I saw the prisoner walking down the steps from the passage leading into the road. He walked down the road, towards Sheffield, and I watched him until he got to the second lamp.'

'Do you recollect anyone passing your back window at that time?'

'Yes, soon after eight I heard Mrs Dyson go by in her clogs. When she got to the closet door I heard her scream loudly. I then opened my back door. Mr Dyson was standing at his own back door and I said to him, 'Go to your wife Mr Dyson.' He then passed me and went directly down the passage to the closet. I then shut the door of my house and went inside.

Almost directly afterwards, I heard two loud bangs and another scream.'

'Before you heard this scream, did you hear the sound of any scuffling,' Foster asked.

'No. I next heard several footsteps in the passage and I opened my door again to see what it was. I saw several people and they appeared to be carrying one man. I could not distinctly see who they were, but they carried Mr Dyson into his house and I there saw him sitting in a chair. He was insensible and blood was streaming down his face.'

Under cross-examination, Mr Lockwood asked, 'Did this man you saw in November, the one you say was Peace, appear just the same as the man you saw in October?'

'Yes,' Mrs Gregory replied.

'Did your husband, in the November time, tell Mr Dyson this man had called asking about him?'

'No, he told him after the first time.'

'You heard your husband make this communication with regard to the 25th of October,'

'Yes.'

'How long after you heard the clogs go by did you hear the scream?'

'Directly after, I might say no more than a minute.'

The next witness to provide testimony was Sarah Colgreaves from Dobbin Hall, which lay about a quarter of a mile from Banner Cross Terrace. 'I remember going to Mr Gregory's shop at about 7:30pm on 29 November 1876, when I met the prisoner walking from the shop. He asked me if I knew who lived in the second house in the terrace, Gregory's is the first house. I told him I didn't know and he asked me if they were strangers. I said they were and he told me the woman that lived there was his mistress. I said he ought to mind what he was saying, particularly to strangers.'

'He asked me if I would mind going to the house and telling the woman an orderly gentleman wished to speak to her,' Mrs Colgreaves continued, 'but I told him he should go himself. When this conversation took place, I had the opportunity to have a good look at the man and I am willing to swear it was the prisoner. I then went on to Gregory's shop. I was there for about ten minutes and, when I left, I saw the prisoner come out of Mr Gregory's passage and go up the road towards Ecclesall.'

Next up was labourer Charles Brassington, who delivered a damning statement. 'At about 8pm on Wednesday 29 November, I was on the road near the Banner Cross Hotel, in Ecclesall Road. The hotel is about thirty yards from Gregory's shop. It was a moonlit night and the prisoner was walking back and forth and he passed me two or three times.'

Brassington went on. 'Afterwards, the prisoner stopped me and asked if I knew of any strangers coming to live in the area. I told him I didn't know and by that time we were standing under a street lamp. Beneath the lamp, he showed me a photograph and some letters. He asked me to read the letters, but I can't read so I took no notice of them. He then said to me, 'I will make it a warm one for these folks before morning, I'll shoot them both.' He then went on towards Gregory's and I left.'

'Did you have the opportunity to get a good look at the man to whom you spoke?' Mr Foster asked.

'I did not pay too much attention to him, but I am sure it was the same man who is in the dock today,' the witness replied.

Dr J.W. Harrison, a Sheffield surgeon, was the next witness. 'I was called to attend to Mr Dyson at around 8:30pm on 29 November. I examined a wound on Mr Dyson's temple that extended upwards, obliquely, into his brain. I remained with Mr Dyson until 10:30pm, when he expired as a result of the wound. The bullet was extracted and given into the custody of Inspector Bradbury.'

Cross-examined by Mr Lockwood, Dr Harrison offered further details. On examining the wound, he had found a slight abrasion on the chin and nose. He did not think those abrasions were likely to have been caused by a blow from a fist, even if the assailant had been wearing a ring. He confirmed he had stated before the Coroner that Mr Dyson had a bruise on his nose and chin as if he had fallen on his face and he was content to stand by that assessment.

When re-examined by Mr Foster, Dr Harrison stated the bullet in the brain had been the cause of death.

The next batch of witnesses were police officers.

Police-Constable George Ward testified as to his examination of the garden opposite Gregory's house, where he had found traces of a man's footprints and, nearby, the bundle of letters produced in court.

Inspector David Bradbury spoke as to the bullet he had received into his custody and it was duly produced in Court. The Inspector said he had spoken to Mrs Dyson on 29 November, as her husband lay dying, and, in consequence of a description she had provided to him, he had initiated a search for Charlie Peace, but had been unable to locate him.

Bradbury produced for the court a photograph provided to him by Mrs Dyson, for the purpose of identifying Peace. Mrs Dyson was recalled to confirm the photograph was of herself and Peace at the Sheffield Fair.

Edward Robinson and Charles Brown of the Metropolitan Police were then called to testify as to their arrest of Peace following a robbery in Blackheath.

The next witness to be called was Mr Woodward, a gun and rifle maker from London. Woodward stated he had examined the rifling of the revolver produced in Court and had found it to have seven grooves. Those groves had corresponded with the markings on the bullet removed from the head of Mr Dyson.

Under cross-examination, Mr Woodward admitted the revolver was of a common type, of which thousands had been imported from Belgium.

This concluded the evidence for the prosecution. Mr Lockwood declined to call any witnesses on behalf of the prisoner.

Mr Campbell Foster then rose to address the jury. He began by saying the cross-examination of Mrs Dyson had clearly been intended to throw doubt upon her evidence and to prejudice the jury against her. Despite this, her testimony had remained unshaken and the counsel for the defence had not dared to call any persons to contradict her testimony.

It was then the turn of Mr Lockwood to address the jury. The lawyer said that, from one end of the country to the other, a cry for blood had been raised, while people whose duty it was to preserve the liberties of their fellow-men had not hesitated, for the sake of the paltry pence they could snatch from the public, to prejudice a fellow creature's life.

Could he, Lockwood asked, hope for even a moment that, though the case had been discussed and canvassed throughout the length and breadth of the land, the jury had not been drawn into the vortex of the discussions?

The defence counsel, fixing his gaze upon them, implored the jury, by the oaths they had taken, not to treat the matter before them as one which they had already determined.

Lockwood then stated that, by attacking the credibility of the evidence provided by Mrs Dyson, he had been simply carrying out his duty, given she had been the only witness who had been present at the time of the shooting. He then asked the jury to look at that evidence with the greatest suspicion.

Mrs Dyson's evidence had a strong bearing upon the case, Lockwood stated, for there was not a soul who could speak as to what really occurred in the passage outside her house other than Mrs Dyson herself and the prisoner at the bar, whose mouth was closed. He was, he said, entitled to the verdict of the jury, because the woman's evidence stood alone and because it had, beyond all doubt, been contradicted on many material points.

The jury had heard his cross-examination, Lockwood said, and might they not consider there had been a struggle and in the course of it the shot had been fired which had caused Mr Dyson's death. If that were so, then the crime was not one of murder.

Lockwood then said he had asked Mrs Dyson, particularly, whether her husband had attempted to catch hold of Peace. Only after he had pressed her repeatedly and she had fenced with him, had he got her to say she was not prepared to swear her husband had not caught hold of him. The position in which the body of the dying man had been found, the lawyer asserted, and other circumstances were all corroborative of the theory it had been during a struggle that the fatal shot had been fired.

It had been noticeable, Lockwood told the jury, after reading out the contents of a card on which they had appeared to place considerable value, the prosecution had declined to enter the card into evidence, presumably because they had been made aware if the card had been entered, they would have also had to enter the letters found with the card. His learned friends, Lockwood said, knew full well that what they, in the exercise of wise discretion, had refused to do, the counsel for the prisoner could not do.

Lockwood then said he next wished to offer that if Mrs Dyson's testimony was to be credited regarding her husband walking down the passage towards Peace, then the bullet would not, as had been shown by the medical testimony, have passed in an upward direction. (This point seemed to completely disregard the vast difference in height between the two men.)

Did not all the evidence, the defence counsel pleaded, point to there having been a struggle, during which the hand of one of the men was being held and pressed towards the head of the man who was holding him. Was it not clear, Lockwood offered, that while the struggle was going on, the revolver went off when Mr Dyson was trying to wrest it away from the prisoner.

If they believed that to have been the case, and they had only the evidence provided by Mrs Dyson to the contrary, Lockwood asked if the jury could really place such implicit faith in such a woman, as to risk the life of a fellow man.

The learned counsel next referred, in detail, to the evidence provided by Mrs Gregory and by Charles Brassington, pointing out the latter had been unable to speak with any great confidence as to dates, or upon the question of identity.

Lockwood then made clear to the jury he did not mean, for a moment, to deny the client on whose behalf he was speaking had been a wild and reckless man. It would be quite possible, the lawyer claimed, for such a man to use threats, under the influence of passion, he did not really intend to carry out. He might, therefore, have made use of some expressions such as those of which Brassington had spoken.

Fixing his eyes upon the jury, Lockwood said he felt sure when they came to consider the weight of the evidence, they would not lay too much stress upon words that might never have been uttered at all.

The defence lawyer asked for a verdict of acquittal on the charge of murder, on the grounds the prosecution had failed, by means of satisfactory testimony and reliable witnesses, to bring the charge home to the prisoner at the bar.

Judge Lopes then addressed the jury. Nobody, he said, regretted more than he did the case had been the subject of so much newspaper coverage. He asked the jury to cast from their minds anything they might have heard or read about the case before they came into court.

The Judge then proceeded to define the crime of murder, which, he said, was the killing of another with malice aforethought, although there were circumstances which might reduce a homicide to the offence known as manslaughter.

Looking next at the testimony offered by Mrs Dyson, the Judge observed that, whatever view the jury might have as to there being any improper familiarity between her and the prisoner, as had been suggested during cross-examination, the case did not rest upon her evidence alone.

The jury had to, Judge Lopes stated, carefully bear in mind that the defence presented had made no attempt to deny the prisoner had been present when Mr Dyson was killed. Moreover, it seemed to have been accepted two shots had been fired, though it had been contended the first shot had been fired merely to frighten Mr Dyson and the second shot had been fired during a struggle that had ensued. These were all matters deserving the consideration of the jury.

With reference to the conduct of Police-Constable Robinson, the Judge said he must be given the greatest credit for the boldness and courage he had displayed in apprehending the prisoner.

Lopes then informed the jury they now had all the facts of the case before them and responsibility for the matter passed from him to them. That they had a most responsible duty to discharge, they were well aware. If they could conscientiously give the prisoner the benefit of any doubt, the Judge explained, then they ought to do so. If, however, they were of the opinion the evidence adduced before them was such as to lead them to the conclusion he had committed murder, and that there was no solid ground upon which the defence could be rested, then they should bear in mind they owed a duty to the community at large.

The Judge implored the jury to not lose sight of the obligation they had incurred by the oaths they had taken.

The jury wasted no time in fulfilling their obligation, retiring to consider their verdict at 7:13pm and returning twelve minutes later, to deliver a unanimous verdict of, 'Guilty.'

The prisoner was asked if there was anything he wished to say as to why sentence should not be passed upon him, to which he replied, in a mumble that could only be picked up by those closest to him, 'Is there any use in me saying anything?'

'Charles Peace,' the Judge said, 'after a most patient trial and after every argument has been urged on your behalf which ingenuity could suggest by your learned counsel, you have been found guilty of the murder of Arthur Dyson by a jury of your fellow-countrymen.'

'It is not my duty,' Lopes continued, 'still less my desire, to aggravate your feelings at this moment by recapitulating any portions of what I fear I can only call your criminal career. I implore you, during the short time which may remain to you in life, to prepare for eternity. I pass upon you the only sentence which the law permits in a case of this kind.'

Donning the dreaded black cap, Judge Lopes proceeded to sentence Charlie Peace to be hung by the neck until dead.

Peace was then led from the dock, bowing politely to his counsel as he walked away to meet his fate.

CHAPTER SEVEN

As he awaited execution, the life story of Charlie Peace was laid out by the newspapers and lapped-up by the ever-eager public.

Charlie Peace was born on 14 May 1832, in Nursery Street, Sheffield.

At the time of Charlie's birth, his father, John Peace, was working as a shoemaker, though he'd been more colourfully employed prior to that time. Having lost a leg in a mining accident, John Peace seems to have decided mining was not a dangerous enough occupation for him and he took a job with Wombwell's Menagerie, where he garnered a reputation as a remarkable trainer of wild animals.

Young Charlie attended school in Sheffield, but was not a particularly attentive pupil, preferring to spend his time making paper ornaments and designing toys, some of which showed promising constructive ingenuity.

On leaving school, Peace took up employment in a rolling mill, but his time there was cut short after he suffered a leg injury from a piece of red-hot steel. The accident rendered him helpless for some eighteen months and left him with a permanent lameness. It was around this time John Peace passed away.

During his recovery, Peace learned to play the violin and by 1853 he had gained sufficient proficiency to join an amateur theatre group, performing under the stage name 'The Modern Paganini' and playing a one-stringed violin.

The criminal career of Charlie Peace began with a robbery in Mount View, Sheffield. It was an inauspicious start however and the novice burglar was caught and jailed for one month.

On his release, Peace began to mingle with some of the more unsavoury characters around Sheffield. He honed his burglary skills and soon became known for his ability to climb the porches of properties in the more affluent parts of the city to gain entry. Following a spree of such robberies in 1854, which netted a large quantity of jewellery, Peace was apprehended and sentenced to four years of penal servitude.

After serving his sentence, Charlie Peace began to wander further afield, continuing to support himself through his joint careers in theft and theatre. In the course of his wanderings, he met Hannah Ward, whom he later married.

Peace's next term in prison, this time sentenced to six years, came after he was captured in Manchester on 11 August 1859, despite a desperate attempt to resist arrest.

The career criminal was released early, in the summer of 1864, and after a brief attempt to start a legitimate business in Sheffield, he returned to Manchester and resumed his life of crime. The result of his return to the robbery game should by now come as no surprise, he was caught and sentenced to ten years of penal servitude.

During this latest period of incarceration, Peace managed to come close to escaping. He procured a rope ladder, while carrying out repair work within the prison, and smuggled it into his cell. Using a home-made saw, he cut a hole in the ceiling but was spotted using the ladder to climb through the gap. Scampering across the rooftop, then along the prison wall, Charlie's bold bid was brought to a sudden halt as he slipped on a loose brick and went crashing through the roof of the prison governor's house.

Trying to make the best of his misfortune, Peace borrowed some of the governor's clothes and waited for a further opportunity, but he was discovered in the governor's bedroom and recaptured. His improved behaviour after this incident saw his sentence eventually being commuted, and he returned to Sheffield in 1872.

Attempting to show he had changed his ways, Peace started up a legitimate business, making picture frames. His children were enrolled in Sunday school and the family took on all the appearance of becoming pillars of the community.

This facade of respectability continued for a while and the family made the fateful decision to move to a better area of Sheffield and re-located to Darnall. Still working as a picture-framer, it was in Darnall he first encountered Mr and Mrs Dyson.

Peace lived in Britannia Road and became noted in the neighbourhood for his collection of rare musical instruments and curiosities of all kinds. He enjoyed inviting people to his house to look over his collections and he began to cultivate the acquaintance of the Dyson family, to the extent he overstepped the mark and his attentions became oppressive.

It was shortly after Mr Dyson took out a warrant against him that another major event in the life of Charlie Peace unfolded.

In July 1876, with the warrant hanging over him, Peace packed up his house-breaking gear and left

Sheffield, bound for Hull and then Manchester. On his arrival in Manchester, he committed a series of burglaries and, on the night of 1 August, he targeted the home of Mr Gatrix of West Point, Whalley Range.

As he entered the grounds and moved towards the house, he was spotted by two police constables, Cock and Beanland. The startled burglar took flight, but as he crossed the garden and jumped over a wall onto the road, he sprung straight into the path of Police-Constable Cock.

The policeman moved to arrest Peace and was met by a warning shot from the burglar's revolver. Taking no heed of the warning, Cock moved forward again, but before he could get hold of his prey he felt the searing heat of a gunshot wound to his chest. As Charlie Peace made his escape, Police-Constable Beanland arrived on the scene, but he would be too late to save the life of his stricken colleague.

Three brothers, who were employed at a nearby market gardener's, were suspected of the murder and two of them, William and John Habron, were subsequently arrested and committed for trial. The brothers had a history with the zealous young policeman and had been overheard threatening to 'do for him' if he was not careful.

John Habron was acquitted, but, although the evidence against him was, at best, flimsy and the Judge had made every attempt to point this out to the jury in his summing-up, William Habron was found guilty of the murder of Police-Constable Cock and was sentenced to death. Following a petition, taken up on his behalf by a group of concerned citizens who believed in his innocence, William Habron's sentence was commuted to penal servitude for life.

With this latest outrage hanging over his head, Charlie Peace returned to Sheffield and his disturbing infatuation with Mrs Dyson resumed.

On 29 November 1876, Peace visited his mother. Later that day, he had an interview with Reverend Newman of Ecclesall Vicarage, to whom he recounted the extraordinary story of his wrongdoings before, even more extraordinarily, claiming the Dyson family had destroyed his life. That same night, Charlie Peace shot and killed Arthur Dyson.

Peace seemed to like living close to the edge and taunting the police. On one occasion, he shared a railway carriage with a police officer and took great delight in reading out to the officer a bill offering a reward of £100 for his own capture.

Early in January 1877, Peace took up lodgings in Nottingham, in a part of the town known as Narrow Marsh. It was here he first made the acquaintance of Mrs Thompson. After living together for a short time in Nottingham, the couple moved to Hull, lodging at the home of a policeman.

While breaking into a villa in Hull, Peace was disturbed by two ladies and two gentlemen. He raced up to the first-floor landing, only to find there were also people coming down the stairs. Drawing his revolver, Peace fired a shot into the ceiling and as everyone dived for cover he made his escape.

On another occasion, the increasingly reckless criminal was stopped by a policeman as he was carrying off the booty from yet another burglary. The constable asked Peace what he was doing and was answered by a shot from the revolver the thief was holding. The policeman, wisely, ran for cover as Peace scurried away.

After returning to Nottingham, Peace and Mrs Thompson were eventually tracked down. After Peace had made an audacious escape along the rooftops, the couple met up and left the provinces, settling in a miserable little home in Stangate Street, Lambeth.

Passing himself off as a dealer in musical instruments, it was in London the criminal career of Charlie Peace attained new heights.

As he was robbing a villa in Denmark Street, Peace came across a safe he was unable to open. Anxious to find out what treasures it contained, the determined burglar sneaked silently upstairs and, as the family lay peacefully sleeping, Peace searched the trouser pockets of the owner of the house and found the key to the safe. Inside, Peace found plate he would later sell in Petticoat Lane for some £250.

Soon afterwards, a burglary in Southampton netted a further £200 in bank notes.

As his wealth begin to grow, Peace decided to relocate, moving to a property in Greenwich better reflecting his circumstances.

Peace arranged for his wife, Hannah, and his son, Willie, to join him and Mrs Thompson in the new property, but living so close together in one house did not work out. Wanting to keep his 'families' together, Peace took on a house in Evelina Road, Peckham, where there was sufficient space for them all to live together under the same roof. The house was semi-detached and had two separate entrances from the main road. The front door opened into a moderately sized hall leading to a large drawing-room with a sitting-room behind.

The house was elaborately furnished, at the expense of the owners of high-class London houses that were systematically relieved of their contents, and improvements to the outside of the property allowed Peace to house his newly purchased pony and trap, enabling him to 'work' further afield.

The two women, unsurprisingly, did not get on particularly well. Mrs Thompson liked a drink and Hannah was never fully able to accept her relationship with Charlie, but they remained loyal to the burglar and he had no fears of treachery as he continued the most successful period of his criminal career.

This unusual, though lucrative, lifestyle remained in place until the capture of Charlie Peace by Police-Constable Edward Robinson, on 10 October 1878.

CHAPTER EIGHT

In the days leading up to his date with the gallows, Charlie Peace took the advice he'd been given by Judge Lopes and began preparing himself for eternity. He requested a meeting with Reverend Littlewood, the Vicar of Darnall, to whom he confessed his version of the truth.

'I wanted to see you,' Peace said, 'to unburden my mind to you. I know I am about to die and I want to take from my conscience some things that weigh heavily upon it. Before I begin, do you believe I am anxious to speak the truth and nothing but the truth?'

'I do,' the vicar replied.

'I was in Manchester in 1876,' Peace stated, 'I was there to work some houses. I went to a place called Whalley Range, I had spotted a house there which I thought I could 'do'. I was respectably dressed, because I made a point of dressing respectably, as the police never think of suspecting anyone who appears in good clothes. In this way, I have thrown the police off guard many a time.'

'On my way to the house that night, I passed two policemen on the road,' Peace continued. 'There were some grounds around the house and my objective was to get into these grounds in the dusk and wait for a chance to get into the house. I walked into the grounds through the gate, but before I was able to begin work I heard a step behind me.'

The confession continued. 'Looking back, I saw it was one of the policemen I had passed on the road. I doubled back to elude him and for a moment I succeeded. Taking a chance, I jumped up onto a wall, but, as I was dropping down on the other side, I all but fell into the arms of the second policeman, who must have been planted for me.'

'This policeman made a grab at me. My blood was up, so I told him, 'You stand back, or I'll shoot you.' He did not step back, so I stepped back a few yards and fired wide of him purposely, to frighten him so I might get away. Now, sir, I want to tell you, and to make you believe me when I say I always made it a rule, during the whole course of my career, never to take a life if I could avoid it.'

'Whether you believe me or not,' Peace went on, 'I never wanted to murder anybody, I only wanted to do what I came to do and get away. It does seem odd that, in the end, I am to be hanged for taking life, the very thing I was so anxious to avoid. I have never willingly or knowingly hurt a living creature. That is why, I tell you, I fired wide at him, but the policeman was as determined a man as myself and, after I had fired wide of him, I observed him take his staff from his pocket.'

'It all happened in a fleeting moment. He was rushing at me and about to strike me and I saw I had no time to lose if I wanted to get away. I then fired a second time, but all I wanted to do was to disable this man carrying the staff, in order that I might get away. I had no intention of killing him. We had a scuffle together and I could not take as careful aim as I might have done. The ball, missing his arm, struck him in the breast and he fell. I know no more, I got away, which was all I wanted.'

'Some time afterwards,' Peace continued, 'I saw in the newspapers certain men had been taken into custody for the murder of this policeman. That interested me. I quite liked to attend trials, so I determined to be present. I left home for Manchester, not telling my family where I had gone. I attended the Manchester Assizes for two days and heard the youngest of the brothers was sentenced to death. The sentence was later reduced to penal servitude for life.'

'Now, sir, some people will say I was a hardened wretch for allowing an innocent man to suffer for my crime, but what man would have done otherwise in my position?' Peace pleaded. 'Could I have done otherwise, knowing, as I did, I should certainly be hanged for the crime? Now that I know I am going to forfeit my own life, and have nothing to gain by further secrecy, I think it right, in the sight of God and man, to clear the young man, who is innocent of the crime.'

Peace moved on. 'That man was sentenced to death on the day before I shot Mr Dyson. I came to Sheffield the morning after the trial and went to Banner Cross that same evening. There is a low wall at the back of the house where the Dyson family lived, which is in Banner Cross Terrace. My objective was to see Mrs Dyson. I stood on the low wall and noticed a light moving about in the bedroom. The blind was up and I could see Mrs Dyson carrying a candle and moving about the room. She was putting her boy to bed.'

'I watched Mrs Dyson for some time, cracked my fingers, then gave a low wolf-whistle to attract her attention, as I had often done before at other places. Mrs Dyson came downstairs. She knew the signal and in response to it she came out. I then got down off the wall and followed her. What did I want there? Simply to get her husband to remove the warrant taken out against me.'

'I was tired of being hunted,' Peace continued. 'If I had got that warrant removed, I would have gone away again. Mrs Dyson became very noisy and used fearful language and threats against me and I got angry. I pulled out my revolver and held it to her face and said, 'Now, you be careful what you are saying to me, you know me of old and you know what I can do. I am not a man to be talked to in that way.' She did not heed what I said and continued her abuse and threats. While this was going on, Mr Dyson hastily made his appearance.'

'As soon as I saw him,' Peace claimed, 'I immediately started down the passage leading to the road. Before I could do so, Mr Dyson seized me and I struggled to get by him. I said, 'Stand back and let me go,' but he did not, so I fired one barrel of my revolver wide of him, to frighten him off. I assure you I purposely fired wide. I could have shot him dead with that first shot if I had chosen to, I was so near to him.'

'Mr Dyson kept his hold of me and we struggled together,' Peace went on, 'and he seemed likely to get the better of me. He had got hold of the arm to which I had strapped my revolver and I knew I had not a moment to spare. I made a desperate effort, wrenched the arm from him, and fired again.'

'It was a life and death struggle, sir, but even then, I did not intend to shoot Mr Dyson. My blood was up and I knew that having fired one shot if I was captured it would be transportation for life. That made me more determined to get off. I fired again, as I told you, but with no intention of killing him.'

'I saw Mr Dyson fall. I did not see where he had been hit or know his wound would prove to be fatal. All that was in my head at the time was to get away and, if we had not struggled, I would have got away without all this. Whatever was said at the trial, I tell you we had a scuffle and for a time Dyson had the best of it.'

'With my revolver, I could have shot him dead at the first, but I did not do so. When I fired the second time, I could not calculate my aim, due to the excitement. If I could have done so, I should have simply disabled him and got away.'

Peace proceeded with his statement. 'After Dyson fell, I rushed into the middle of the road and stood there for several moments. I hesitated as to what I should do. I felt disposed at first, to go back and help Dyson up, not thinking he was fatally wounded, but people began to gather. I was greatly agitated and I decided to make my escape.'

'I jumped over the wall on the other side of the road and got away. As I did so, the packet of letters fell from my pocket. I call God to witness, sir, I did not kill Mr Dyson intentionally and I most solemnly swear that in shooting at him, I did not intend to murder him. If anyone thinks about it for a moment, they will see I never intended murder when I went to Banner Cross. If I had meant to murder Mr and Mrs Dyson, or either of them, I knew the place well enough. All I had to do was go to the door, walk in and shoot them both where they were sitting.'

'Do you think, sir, if I had gone there to murder Mr Dyson, I would have allowed myself to have been seen by so many people?' Peace asked. 'Of course, I do not deny I took Mr Dyson's life, as it turned out, but I did not go there with the intention of doing it. It was as unintentional a thing as ever was done. It would never have been done if I had not been interrupted in trying to get Mrs Dyson to induce her husband to withdraw the warrant, and if Mrs Dyson had not been so determined to get me into trouble and prevent my getting away.'

The seemingly unlucky little gunman, who had now claimed to have accidentally shot and killed two people, closed the interview by asking Littlewood to hear him pray. For some twenty minutes, he poured out fervent petitions for mercy and prayed for the souls of Mr Dyson and Police-Constable Cock, whose lives he had so recklessly ended.

In light of Peace's confession to the murder of Police-Constable Cock, William Habron would eventually be released from prison, on 18 March 1879.

Charlie Peace was executed within the precincts of Armley Prison, in Leeds, on 25 February 1879.

On the eve of his execution, the convicted murderer had spent the day speaking with his relatives and joining them in earnest prayer. Peace had said a prayer for each individual member of his family, before praying for the relatives of the two men he had killed, for William Habron, who had been sentenced to death for one of the murders, and, finally, for himself.

After his family had left, the grief-stricken prisoner had been visited by the prison chaplain, Reverend Cookson, who had remained with him until the late evening. Peace had then been visited by the prison

Governor, Mr Keene. He had assured the Governor he was truly repentant and had informed him, somewhat optimistically, he was sure he was bound for Heaven.

Reverend Cookson had then returned and spoken with Peace into the early hours of the morning before the exhausted prisoner had managed to catch a few hours of sleep.

At 6:15am, Peace had devoured a hearty breakfast of bacon, eggs, toast and tea.

As the hands of the prison clock crawled towards 8am, the doom-laden tolling of the prison bells saw the execution party emerge from within the wing of the prison housing Charlie Peace. The group was led by Governor Keene, who was followed by Under-Sheriff Gray, Reverend Cookson and the manacled figure of Charlie Peace.

Two warders were on hand to support the prisoner, but they were not required as Peace walked towards the gallows with steady strides. Although understandably pale and haggard looking, it seemed he had come to terms with his fate and Peace betrayed no visible signs of fear.

As Peace took his place on the scaffold, the hangman, William Marwood, bound his legs and placed a rope around his neck. As the executioner was about to place a white cover over his head, Charlie Peace began to speak.

'God have mercy upon me, Lord have mercy upon me, Christ have mercy upon me,' Peace pleaded. Thinking he had finished, Marwood moved forward again with the white cover, but the prisoner had more to say.

Turning to look at four reporters who were standing close by, Peace said, 'You gentlemen reporters, I wish you to notice the few words I am going to say to you. I know my life has been base and bad. I wish you to ask the world after you have seen my death, what man could die as I die if he did not die in the fear of the Lord. Tell all my friends I feel sure they have forgiven me and I am going to the Kingdom of Heaven, or else to that place prepared for us to rest until the great Judgement Day.'

'I have no enemies that I feel to have on this earth,' Peace continued, 'I wish all my enemies, or those would-be enemies, I wish them well and I wish them to come to the Kingdom of Heaven at last. Amen. Say my last wishes and my last respects are to my dear children and to their dear mother. I hope no person will disgrace them by taunting them or jeering at them on my account, but that you will have mercy upon them. God bless you, my children. Goodbye, Heaven blesses you. Oh, my Lord God, have mercy upon me. Amen.'

As Marwood finally placed the cover over his head, Peace was heard to ask for a drink of water. His request was ignored and, as the chaplain came to the end of his short service with the words, 'Lord Jesus, receive his spirit,' the hangman released the bolt and Charlie Peace dropped to his near instantaneous death.

Marwood had developed the 'long drop' technique of hanging, which ensured the condemned man's neck was broken instantly at the end of the drop, allowing death by asphyxiation while unconscious, rather than the previous 'short drop' method of slow death by strangulation.

At 11am, Mr Malcolm, the coroner, held an Inquest, after which the body of Charlie Peace was buried within the grounds of Armley Prison.

In the days leading up to his execution, Peace had written a number of letters, sixteen in all, offering advice to his family and friends. He had asked that the chaplain send them out, on his behalf, on the day of his execution, so they would be considered to have been 'sent from the scaffold'.

Peace also designed and sent out a funeral card, which read: 'In memory of Charles Peace, who was executed in Armley Prison, Tuesday, 25 February 1879, aged 47, for that I done but never intended.'

OTHER BOOKS BY THE AUTHOR

True Crimes: Ladykillers
True Crimes That Shaped Scotland Yard
True Crimes in Victorian Times: Murder in Pocock's Fields
Edinburgh: A Capital City

Printed in Great Britain
by Amazon